Simeon

Simeon

A Greater Reality

Julie Rogers

FIRST EDITION
First Printing, 2014

Unless otherwise noted, Scripture quotations are taken from the *New Scofield Reference Bible, Authorized King James Version of the Holy Bible*, Oxford University Press, Inc., 1967.

HOLY BIBLE: NEW INTERNATIONAL VERSION® (NIV). © 1973, 1978, 1984 by International Bible Society. Used by permission of Zondervan Publishing House. All rights reserved.

Library of Congress Cataloging-in-Publication Data
Rogers, Julie, 1959—
Simeon: A Greater Reality/Julie Rogers. — 1st ed.

xxvi, 272 p., |c22.86 cm.

ISBN 978-0-615-97233-6 (sc)
ISBN 978-0-692-38674-3 (e)

Printed and bound North America by
Lulu.com

10 9 8 7 6 5 4 3 2 1

For my husband

Acknowledgments

It's always difficult to specify acknowledgments, when, upon concluding a lengthy endeavor, you realize that every single person, event, or circumstance you've ever encountered has somehow contributed to how you think and who you are. There are no stray marks. The pulses of many, many souls are in this book.

The additional effort of a primal few have afforded this book life, and those I wish to thank are: the initiative, Simeon Peter himself, my mentor Elizabeth Thorson, my editor June Ford, the supportive team at Lulu, and my intuitive brothers and sisters, you know who you are. And not to forget my family: my husband, my son, and my parents. Grace to you all.

Contents

Foreword

How It Began

I've always been curious about many things in life, particularly the unknown. At one time I believed that by completely engaging in virtually every opportunity that came along, I was not only learning more about all the things I didn't know, but also experiencing life to its fullest. However, my full-tilt approach sometimes only served as an energy drain—to me and to others around me.

Some people have alluded that I am a Jill-of-all-trades, or talented in several arenas. But at times I've felt like life just turned into a great big revolving door—one that began with numerous hours in a career consultant's office, leading later still toward many false career starts. That's the con side of things. The pro side is, even today I approach life from a broad base and an interdisciplinary viewpoint. I've loved and dabbled in many things—fine arts, music, foreign language, psychology, theology, nursing, athletics, martial arts, modeling, dance, journalism, screen-writing, theater, film—a plethora of entrepreneurial ventures that, to be sure, has probably raised a few eyebrows. This prodigious list is only an attempt to help you, the reader, understand the world-view from which I came, the backdrop of experiences which led me to channeling this incredible entity and energy named Simeon Peter.

Rewind about nine years before I started this book. I was

carrying on in my full-tilt manner at warp speed. I'd remarried, had my first child, and started my own small production company—when life as I'd always known it came crashing down around me. At the time it didn't seem to be anything more than painful. Later, I began to see those ten bone-crunching months as significant. I was well-acquainted with pain. Once a ballet dancer, later a competitive endurance athlete, body builder, and martial artist, I'd weathered my share of broken bones, tendonitis, torn ligaments, and corrective surgeries. I'd also had three intra-abdominal surgeries for a congenital digestive disorder. I was well versed with various kinds and levels of pain and how to push past them. But this pain—nothing compared to it. To say I was being repeatedly skewered through from behind with a serrated carving knife might begin to describe it. But the pain was elusive and untimely in every way. When my son was just a baby, this pain was episodic in nature—maybe once or twice a year. Six years later the pain came on suddenly with a vengeance, and apparently to stay. At the time, the particular location and pattern of onset didn't correspond to any old injuries, somatic dysfunction, musculoskeletal distress, or even present as referred pain. My husband, being a doctor, naturally had me seeing every specialist—spinal, gastrointestinal, neurological, gynecological. As test after test revealed nothing physiologically wrong, my despair grew.

AN INTRODUCTION TO MYSTICISM

Aside from a brief literary examination of early Christian mystics, I hadn't given much thought to what mystics do, or how they do it. At one of my lowest points I contacted a regionally renowned osteopathic physician, who also found no exact diagnosis, but was in tune with something—well, different. I walked out of his office with a book, Carolyn Myss's *Anatomy of the Spirit.* Myss, a mystic and medical intuitive, tours internationally as a speaker on spirituality and mysticism.

Could pain this intense have purely spiritual roots? At the time, I found this suggestion somewhat confounding, and, quite frankly, insulting. But, among the many, many other realities I was about to discover, this was at least partly true.

At home, I curled up in a large blue glider rocker, its post-back faded from my constant use of a heating pad, with my knees rolled into my chest—the only position in the only seat I'd been able to tolerate for months—and read. I realized I had one of two choices. I could continue steadily escalating my usage of prescription narcotics in order to be able to function some of the time, a window that was closing rapidly with each passing week. Or I could follow my hunch that contacting a medical intuitive was just the thing I needed to do. By Memorial Day it became clear to me that I was fast losing any ability to enjoy life, so I e-mailed intuitive Elizabeth Thorson. When Elizabeth saw me having a reincarnational, or past-life, injury, I was even more buffaloed. *So I'd had other lives, but I just couldn't remember them? How many other warp-speed vocational experiences did I manage to make in those lifetimes?* I jokingly asked myself. To someone as invested into dumping every achievement possible into the only lifetime I'd assumed I had, this idea didn't seem to have legs. I didn't believe in reincarnation. I liked Elizabeth—and as a gifted clairvoyant and emergency room RN, she understood my need for intellectual validation. She understood how a backlog of childhood religious beliefs supported by very conservative western theology had me scrambling for a foothold in this unfamiliar territory. (Elizabeth, incidentally, would mentor me over the next ten years.)

I dutifully followed the suggestions she gave, which resulted in complete healing. I also began studying and practicing Qigong energy healing, Traditional Chinese Medicine, and Tui Na (Qigong massage). I'd heard about channeling, but my interests at the time lay more in learning everything I could about energy healing. I began remembering how to value small pleasures—the way cool water feels when it runs through one's fingers, the way birds sing at daybreak. During those months of healing, I became aware for the first time of what I'll call "intrinsic soul value," or Being, and its quiet, unequivocal greatness— and yes, over all my personal achievements I'd acquired during this lifetime. I also began to realize that any human world view—no matter how seemingly expanded—truly experiences only ten percent of reality according to quantum theory, when perceived through the five physical senses alone. I thought long and hard about that. *Ten percent.* What is reality? And why am I here, both blessed and limited by such a body?

Given the possibility of reincarnation, then, I was coming to see that my journey toward healing most likely involved remembering and trusting some metaphysical realities and intuitive abilities I'd obviously forgotten. A huge chunk of my day-to-day belief system was uprooted and scrutinized, and much of it would not be replanted into my life in the same way. A brave new world had just opened up before me, and yes, still another series of choices and challenges—but a journey I somehow knew I wouldn't regret.

Introduction

A Skeptic's Acceptance

A series of decisions inevitably lead me to channeling—but not for a while yet. I was busy once again, studying the healing arts. I'd been pain free for about six months, and evermore determined to understand just how and why my healing had occurred. I was also becoming familiar with author Helen Schuchman, and altogether fascinated by the manner in which she received *A Course in Miracles* through distinct, clairaudient dictation. Schuchman also presented astounding material regarding reality versus illusion, Being versus ego. At one time in my life I might've sat back and contemplated Schuchman and her channeled work as interesting, but not necessarily practical. But now, day after day, I was experiencing its truth myself.

I was intrigued by several other new age authors, mediums, and channelers, but I was still clinging to a good bit of fear of what I'd once viewed as possessions, dissociation, or psychic invasion. I was also concerned about the credibility or validity of channeled material. My religious upbringing had me believing that all channeling was the outworking of demonic possession, borderline personality disorder, or at best, dissociative identity disorder under development. Though I had released religious intolerance to a certain degree, I'd also spent many years as a serious theology student with conservative skepticism about dangers of the occult. What's more, I had a closet full of research notes, several years' worth, in fact—which detailed exactly how this demonic possession could occur.

I also knew any number of psychologists and hypnotherapists who were highly uncomfortable with the possible subjective filtering of information and subconscious projection that can occur unintentionally while in trance states. Some people have committed heinous crimes because voices told them to do so and that, too, certainly gave me pause. Even a number of holistic and interfaith theologians I knew, regardless of their personal mysticism or openness, still drew the line when it came to channeling. It was easy for me to see how some would overlook what in reality is a very responsible approach and label channelers in general as loose cannons. Knowing these things made me take a few steps back.

CLAIRAUDIENCE 101

Elizabeth had identified clairaudient ability as one of my untapped intuitive resources, however. I spent some more time reading in the blue rocker—by then, I'd donated the heating pad to charity—devouring book after book about mediumistic abilities and experiences. I read most of Jane Roberts's *Seth* books in one summer, as well as the works of Esther and Jerry Hicks, Sonaya Roman, James Van Praagh, Deepak Chopra, Allison DuBois, Jon Klimo, and others.

I tentatively began comparing some experiences of my own— the little daily helper messages like, "one in the hold," when I'd forgotten a sock in the clothes dryer, or catching a glimpse of our little dog Sydne walking through our house a week after she'd died, or receiving a startling vision of a friend on oxygen several months before her illness became symptomatic.

The daily helper messages, as I understood them to be, were forms of open channeling, or receiving information from several possible nonphysical sources. From early on I felt that channeling had much broader implications than classic channeling, where a named nonphysical source claims responsibility for the information coming through a channel who goes into deep trance. Solutions that seem to come from nowhere, inspired words or thoughts, even a sense of knowing or sudden enlightenment, I believe, are all forms of channeling. Many of the channeled messages coming to me made sense—but an even greater number didn't.

I also felt concerned that I might be producing nothing more than reconstituted information I'd pulled from one author or the next, or fragments of my eroded belief system. Sometimes I felt like I didn't catch a complete transmission, as it were, or certain combinations of words came through that just didn't make sense. I certainly didn't want to mislead myself or anyone else. For this reason I continued to contact Elizabeth periodically, a little unsure how I should proceed. As always, she continued to emphasize my need to surrender and trust—that this was the true problem—as well as my need to relieve myself of the idea that all sixth-sense communication had to be delivered in neatly wrapped packages with bows on top.

Snatches of one- and two-word impressions often came to me when performing repetitive or nominal household tasks, which I came to understand as a form of self-hypnosis. I'd be tooling away at something—always thinking, yes—often quietly ruminating over a past personal encounter, a future task at hand, or even a problem, and some clairaudient communication would come across as an interruption: one, two, or even several words superimposed over my thoughts. Sometimes the words that came across applied to my thoughts at hand, but often they did not. Thus, the words seemed very often to emerge indistinct from my own voice, and on a different train of thought, about an entirely different subject.

During the hypnagogic and hypnopompic states—the states of consciousness right before drifting to sleep and becoming awake—I found clairaudient communication to be its loudest and clearest. These fell into every category: a sweet, grandmotherly type who woke me once at five a.m. sharp with a lilting, singsong "Good Morning!" to a resounding baritone military type who got me stirring and laughing one day with his booming "Put your feet on the floor!" Certainly these examples contributed to a growing pool of interesting encounters and great entertainment. But I had an even stronger desire to understand these abilities, to use them to help others in some way—perhaps even in the way I'd been helped—to overcome physical illness or disease.

The Friendly Skies

One evening, instead of the crusty baritone or huggable grandma, I got a neck adjustment. No words. I told my husband it felt like very gentle craniosacral work. My neck felt great, and I chalked up the experience to nonphysical osteopaths, teasing my husband that "this sky-friendly manipulation sure is a lot easier to take than what they taught you in medical school."

When I read about Esther Hicks's similar experience in *The Law of Attraction,* my hair stood on end. Hicks had experienced odd movements of her neck during meditation and had soon realized she was making cursive letters in the air with her nose. These, for her, were the first channeling attempts of Abraham. I realized the moment I read about Hicks's experience that perhaps some entity or entities wanted me to go beyond the one- and two-word phrases. My struggle to accept what I was hearing or sensing—often because I didn't know how to interpret what I'd received—was probably my biggest barrier at the time.

Simeon addresses this problem on several occasions, which I believe offers invaluable insight for anyone who may be interested in channeling but finds the initial process as elusive as I did. So, for the moment, I decided to stop analyzing and *just do it.* Who knows, I thought, I might end up with something extremely helpful for myself or for others. At the very least, with practice my abilities might improve, I thought—though I certainly did not commence with very high hopes.

FIRST CONTACT

MAY 6

Perhaps it is proximity to water, which is historically linked with stronger psychic connections, but as first contact would happen with me, it occurred in the bathroom on an ordinary afternoon. I'd been attempting to more directly and deliberately channel for a week, sitting with my eyes closed at a computer keyboard. Most of what I'd received was a string of hiccuped words that read like two radio advertisements playing simultaneously. In fact, that's what it felt like—being caught between frequencies. So I'm tooling around, shuffling around little piles of hair bands, toiletries, and teeth whitener on the bathroom countertop, ruminating over my sky-friendly neck adjustment and wondering just who, if anyone, I was channeling. Clairaudient information had been running at an all-time low lately; I only had one client at the moment, and my Aries-challenged self-esteem wasn't feeling too great about that, either. So I was keeping my stir-crazy self occupied sorting through hair bands when Simeon Peter made his entrance.

Peter.

This was a barely discernible clairaudient burp, riding just above my own turbulent thoughts. I almost didn't catch it.

Oh, I reacted. *I don't really know how I feel about that right now. In fact, I'm not sure I even heard that at all. Simon Peter?* In a reading for my husband three years prior, Elizabeth had gotten an impression of Simon Peter around him. This seemed to correspond to my husband's work as an osteopathic physician and possibly to my evolving work as a healer. That must be it, I thought. I was just remembering what Elizabeth had said.

I likened channeling a prominent Biblical entity, the "father of the church," to someone believing he or she happened to be the reincarnation of Joan of Arc or Elvis. It was too convenient for me to trust. I would've been far more comfortable hearing a really wacko name like *Zedlevor*. So I decided to push the envelope a little. "I don't believe you," I said. "In fact, maybe you better follow that up with another name that lets me know who you really are, if you're saying you're really Peter." Since I still struggled with two-way clairaudient communication, I fully did not expect any answer to my question. And, couched in that kind of distrust, it was no wonder. So I went back to rearranging my bathroom countertop.

Simeon.

That got my attention. If I'd heard—or thought I'd heard, Simon, I would've dismissed the entire experience as my own wishful overthinking. Because I first expected nothing, or my own imaginary best Simon, Apostle, or Saint—the word Simeon took me by surprise. I was convinced, you see, that Simon or Saint would have been a full-blown reproduction of my own thought process. I went online and looked up the name. Simeon, the dictionary said, was an older Hebrew derivation of Simon. The Biblical Peter, I knew, was said to have answered to both. I can't say my attitude was the most conducive to receptivity of any name, let alone Simeon Peter. My relationship with him began, therefore, out of my struggle to accept what I'd heard.

For months I maintained the same come-again, go-again defensive posture concerning what Simeon Peter would say. Underneath it all, I discovered, was my own deep-seated fear of being wrong. This defensive posture would slowly peel away as the months rolled by. And I would later learn that it is no coincidence the older derivation of Simon, or Simeon, means, "to be heard."

In the mind are pathways like an early rosebud—
closed, yet ever ready to bloom to perfection.

—Simeon Peter

.

Chapter One

Automatic Typing

APRIL 30

About a week before first contact, I'd sat down at a computer keyboard for a first official session, attempting to record those first incoherent words using automatic typing. These notes were my preface: We're off to a good start, for while I may harbor some preconceptions, I have no earthly idea what I'm writing about. Two nights ago, I received a quick phrase that I would be writing something regarding "reviewing origins from which you came."

When I sit down and quiet my own mental chatter long enough to focus on my breath, it does seem that I eventually receive a few words as being dictated to me, which I then type on my computer.

This field is a network of lines central that go behind open judgment.

I still feel that my clairaudient receptivity is only average, although I've been actively clairaudient for nearly ten years. Clairaudience falls into two categories: perception of voices, tones, or noises not audible to the human ear, or mental impressions from an "inner mental ear" without any auditory impressions. By the spring, I was mainly familiar with the former way of receiving, and I habitually heard information in two- and three-word bursts.

Clairaudient receptivity, unlike telepathy, predisposes one to open channeling, or receiving messages from disembodied spirits or the deceased. To act as an open channel—to receive information in two- or three-word phrases as I always have—is a very arduous way, however, to receive more lengthy material. I've wondered how this way of receiving might progress. When an entity steps forward and takes initiative to identify him or herself as a teacher (classic channeling), it naturally follows that a more efficient way of communication will develop. And I trust that as my ability matures, errors or corrections that need to be made to this material will also be channeled to me.

MAY 7

A week later, I'm sitting down for session two.

They went further like it from time to time; they went back and forth somewhat like the one before.

MAY 9

And session three.

We are noticed in comfort: a fish swims, birds feed themselves, and the cycle continues. Start looking for this. Connect and hold. He brings water to give them both. Because it washes against them, they survive. Total life water brings to its carrier. The air speed—that none of that is written—is mapped.

This little boy will save many. Watch how he writes. In front of him especially is a train of thought he must follow. Be the yielder. Give him room. There is space for you both. Yield.

In this session, I had a strong impression that "he" meant God, or of the essence of God. It was only an impression at the time. Months later I was teaching my son about the components of the water cycle. It suddenly became crystal clear to me that those microscopic droplets of moisture in the air we breathe constantly "wash" us—that we are essentially surrounded by and immersed in water throughout our lives. Without water in our breath, we wouldn't survive.

THE MISSING COMPONENT

MAY 13

I'll attempt a session a little earlier in this evening, before we're all headed to bed. It's about 8:40 p.m., and my left shoulder hurts, so I'll see how long I can focus. Though the debilitating back pain has never returned, I've been exhibiting what seems to be some bursitis in my left shoulder for more than a year. (I would later learn that this disorder developed out of my inability to trust my own expressive traits and had originated in my Vishuddha chakra, or neck).

For joy.

The voice just didn't come, and I finally gave up entirely on that session. Then a series of vacations interrupted. In the meantime, I read Jane Roberts's *Seth Speaks*. I was so deeply impressed with this work, I began to have serious doubts about what more could be added to such depth—similar to the feelings I had regarding *A Course in Miracles*. I can only suppose that, as Seth indicated in Roberts's writing—with the continuing expansion and expression of souls, the inspirational material coming to us will be ever changing. I would think it would be utterly useless to merely repeat in any fashion what has been so beautifully said before, unless part of it has been terribly misinterpreted, overlooked, or forgotten.

I didn't attempt another session until June. The messages remained terse and confusing. I considered the session on the thirteenth to be *Simeon incommunicado* until later, when Simeon gave me directives for increasing my own personal joy in order to assist in communicating with him.

JUNE 9

After the last session, you might say I come with a certain amount of apprehension. Will I encounter only silence again?

Reminder: those who come too late or by themselves, historically speaking, find purpose.

June 10

The next evening, already later than I'd intended on sitting for a session, I thought I'd listen in for a few minutes. The house is quiet. I'm remembering that *A Course in Miracles,* as well as other material I've been reading lately, repeatedly reinforces that the world does not come to meet us from without, but begins within. There are bothersome gnats over the computer screen, and the dogs are howling at the train once again. Perhaps I am still too consumed with what I see and experience as the "world without." I only type:

Sentencing occurs even right now. In the mind are pathways like an early rosebud, closed, yet ever ready to bloom to perfection.

Changing Spaces

June 12

It's Friday at 8:48 p.m., and I've decided that my shoulder would give me less grief if I use a laptop. I've also moved the sessions to a small cabin behind our house. The cabin has a noisy AC window unit, but I have a hunch nonetheless that conditions might be more conducive to receiving here, where I've practiced Qigong on a regular basis. I've often remarked that this cabin feels like "home" to me.

Disbursement: Today you are seated in the chair even at night. We request more light. First thing we need you to do: release. I would think you might try this again at nighttime. It is good for you to face truth, a good reaction. See this as looking through a telescope—as if this is your vision.

These previous examples are but a few of the early short sessions I completed during the first four months. I've included only a handful of them at the outset of this book so readers will understand that I didn't just wake up one morning, leap out of bed, and find myself recording volumes of orderly and systematic notes. Much of the early sessions were almost incoherent and reminded me of trying to listen to three or four conversations going on at once. The development of the ability to attune to a single voice, or train of thought, took time, concentration, and practice.

When I say *concentration,* I'm talking about the shift in focus that began by first becoming aware of my own incessant mental chatter, then developing the ability to allow my self-talk to be quieted. In eastern culture and spiritual practices, this shift is often found through meditation, known as *kenosis*, or self-emptying. The creed of Japanese martial arts (adapted from Isshin-Ryu karate) is, "I come to you with only karate, empty hands."

Throughout history, a common thread in many eastern and western religious teachings is the mystique surrounding shifts in consciousness (and often, the better fortune or emotional relief noted thereafter), when a man relaxes his grip on what he feels is critical, abandons all hope in external circumstances, throws in the towel, or allows what come what may. Getting oneself out of the way can be the most difficult task.

During the session on June 12, I relaxed just enough to enter into a light trance state where I was actually unaware of the words I was typing. There was a flow to it. I became unaware of my surroundings. I let go.

And yet, I had at least two more weeks of what I viewed at the time as incomprehensible.

JUNE 15

Pace yourself. There needs to be a vacuum, and so for you to continue.

JUNE 20

Monumental lessons will happen along directly open pathways. We quite become what we've entered into in hope in that special realm.

From reading about other intuitives, I knew that receiving strange, incongruous phrases is not at all uncommon. I kept trying to understand how to make the leap from hearing or knowing a few words to complete sentences as they came across. As a writer familiar with stringing words together, my greatest fear was overwriting what Simeon intended to say, particularly when I disagreed with his word usage.

WANTED: LIGHT

Then something began to change. I began having what I'll call impressions of thoughts that crossed my mind during my attempts to receive clairaudiently, word for word, what Simeon Peter was trying to say. I guess you could say I had three conversations going on in my head: my own, a word or two here and there clairaudiently, and this stream of thought that sort of took off on its own. At first these thought impressions didn't seem to fit or work as lead offs, or what I deemed appropriate beginnings of sentences. But I decided to listen primarily to these thought impressions anyway—and to trust that they were as bona fide as the rest. When I retired at night—when I was most relaxed—I let these thought impressions flow, whether they turned out sense or nonsense. I didn't try to make mental notes; I just listened. I felt there was something helpful in this kind of process, like surfing television channels for the right program, or switching radio bandwidths for other frequencies.

Sometimes I felt like I was listening to a radio at a very low volume that was just off the station. I also experienced headaches clustered around the pineal gland, or what the Indian chakra system refers to as the *third eye*. From what I've experienced, the ability to channel improves with these and several other physiologic and esoteric shifts. For example, energetic blockages from misalignment and somatic dysfunction originating in the neck, spine, or legs can hinder the channel. Stimulation of the pineal gland occurs during clairvoyant development. Changes in the limbic system have also been recorded during trance states. On the esoteric level, thought forms travel to the channel on something like carrier waves, or sinusoidal waveforms that oscillate much faster than human speech. My frequency didn't start out matching Simeon's, which he refers to in the session on June 12.

I believe the *light* that Simeon spoke about at the time was the constitution of my morphogenetic field or light field, an organizational structure that consists of far more than just visible flesh and blood. In these fields that we also call human souls exist reincarnational wave signatures that oscillate at certain tonal frequencies. When considering a human being as a field, a human being also has a human mental field and consciousness that exist within the human brain as well as without it. Morphogenetic fields are just as real as galactic and solar gravitational fields, electromagnetic fields, molecular fields, atomic fields, or quantum-matter fields. When we break down human essence, or the human field, to its subatomic structures, we discover that we are made of light. Science measures light fields in terms of heat, or vibratory thermal energy. We each carry this energetic signature of light, and its intensity varies according to how we live. The ancient practice of Qigong teaches that our Wei Qi, or human essence, originated from light, or vibratory energy from the Divine. One's vibratory thermal energy, or light field, is enhanced (or reduced) by dietary habits, exercise, exposure to climate and toxins, thought patterns, the emotional state of the psyche, and spiritual continuity.

Suffice to say, a simple misplaced belief like, "*I can't trust this until I fully understand exactly how it works*," could conceivably create such a block in one's psyche that a person could die of a bacterial infection while holding a bottle of antibiotics. Relatively small, but unresolved issues with trust can impair light transmission, and I've learned that these issues don't always follow our commonly held ideas about what it means to be spiritual or to follow a spiritual path. Issues with light cannot be neatly divided into "good" or "bad" behavior. The belief systems that influence our behavior most significantly are likely ones that we are least aware of. A backlog of pervasive, unconscious thought patterns—ones that we may not even put into words—those can represent belief systems that impair light transmission the most. And life has a way of mirroring our deepest beliefs to us, whether we see them or not.

Mystic Hildegard of Bingen is quoted saying, "Why do you live without passion, why do you live without blood?" Her writings in her medieval classic *Physica* concerning the medicinal properties of plants convey her awareness that when man consumes food, he consumes the photosynthesis that created it so, namely, the conversion of light to food. When man eats food, he is light eating light. So to live without passion—to lose the ability to enjoy life—is to lack light. If a man refuses food or cannot enjoy food when he needs it, he is refusing light. If he can no longer feel joy, his light is diminished.

So, for the remainder of June, you might say I was under light development—becoming increasingly aware of the mental activity rolling around in my head and whether that was conducive or counterproductive to light.

In early July, I received instructions about where to sit in the cabin.

JULY 9

The right way is to come. The coordinate point is just to the left of the table behind you.

Coordinate points are vectors for dynamic energy, specific locations scattered throughout the earth's surface that are more conducive to spiritual contact. These points may also match certain degrees latitude and longitude, with many located around coastal areas or areas near water. We were living pretty far inland at the time. However, the space indicated was possibly located over an underground spring. I changed where I sat in the cabin according to Simeon's instructions, and we were off and running.

JULY 19

Okay. An opening can come from childlike attention, and release, and joy. You must share this joy, and keep your joyful focus, your smile upon it. A tunnel of research would not bring you to this place. Before you go any further, take the time to realign your back. When you call his [Simeon's]* name, he is aware of you.

Right now he is preparing for a greater release of all that he can send your way. Wait for it. Continue shifting slightly until he finds you and you find him.

[*Throughout, bracketed text placed in Simeon's text are clarifications by Julie Rogers; parentheses in Simeon's text are clarifications by Simeon; parentheses in Julie Rogers's text are clarifications by Julie Rogers.]

A dream is a fundamental case study of each individual soul, so to speak. It is a thimble of reality in time; a modicum of reality outside of time.

During that session, it felt like someone put a vibrating headband around my head. Immediately after the session, I moved to another place in the room. It felt different. I returned to the coordinate point, and I felt the band around my head again. I moved slightly in front of this space. The band was gone.

Also, it's interesting to note that in this session, Simeon was introduced in the third person, as if the information was coming from a separate entity who was paving the way for him.

JULY 23

I'm sitting precisely under this same spot as I go into the next session, but I'm not feeling a headband around my head tonight. I've thought about the suggestion that a good way to induce a session is by focusing on childlike joy.

My husband suggested that my childlike place usually occurs when I am recognized for some hard-earned achievement, but I reminded him about the baby birds that my son and I had rescued earlier this spring, and he said yes, with animals also—there is this childlike appreciation and joy. So I spent maybe a minute visualizing the sea turtle my son and I had watched one night, remembering its comical paddling rhythm.

Although I had doubts about how this imaginary and emotive induction would work, a breakthrough was just minutes away.

Chapter Two

Breakthrough

JULY 23

The following session in late July marked the beginning of comprehensible sessions, as well as the end of incoherency or silence. I'm including most of the sessions and notes taken in the same manner up to the end of June. For clarity, I've added some punctuation and parenthetical information. Also, occasionally I've divided longer, rambling passages into parts, while making a conscious decision not to extensively edit text where Simeon uses odd word constructions or apparently manufactured words or concepts. Much of the editing also addressed my own typos or misspelled words. Where Simeon has a tendency to ramble in some places, I've let it stand, realizing that this might be his own effort to identify complex or prospective discoveries with simpler or even symbolic examples. In spite of this, he identifies himself as not one to mince words.

Tonight we will continue with dreams. The dream state is in a fashion after a reality of its own. No one can partake in such a state without describing the world to him or herself all over again. It is a place, a field of dreams, if you will, where enlightenment of the profoundest nature occurs.

To wallow in one's self-pity during the waking hours will unfold dreams of obscurity; nightmares are reserved for stronger emotions. Self-pity is the cruelest form of separation a mind can achieve. It sees oneself as an antithesis of life; it is dead in its own right before one's "time" is up. Time—as you know I speak of—is only the conclusion of all things in my reality; therefore self-pity has just cornered a figment of your imagination. It is not real. (I will show you a greater reality in just a moment.) You may think that this [channeled material] *flows only from your own thoughts, what you have acquired from reading, reading, reading the past three years—or for that matter your entire life—but I am here to show you that there is more than meets the eye (pardon my pun).*

Your favor is requested; try to loosen up your elbows just a bit and let this flow now.

In March of next year, you will have [written] *a book. I know that this you find hard to envision or believe. But this will happen.*

Just allow the thoughts to flow, as if you were saying them with your own mind. Do not fret that you should be channeling something other than your own thoughts. The impediment of your own blabber *will not course through your veins much longer. You are a good student. You have tried very hard. Now you have to let even more go: Let's get started.*

My name is Simeon Peter. Peter, *which I gave you first, was yet another test of your belief, your willingness to trust, and that you were not* [trusting].

Simon *would've led you down a different path. So I therefore* chose Simeon, *the ancient Hebrew, fast past* [fast before, a long time before] *Aramaic, to delight you in that you have found yet an older soul than the Biblical* Simon. *We are one in the same, but you would not have dared uttered a thought since about channeling, if I had announced myself as* Simon. *Trust me on that.*

In the beginning God did create [Genesis 1:1], *and is still creating, even as your fingers type upon this page. Never forget that. Creation means freedom, for all souls, all spirits, all nations. For as energy creates and recreates, life goes on. And life is free to become that which it would rather-be. For life is always in the midst of becoming what it would rather-be. Have you not heard?* [Isaiah 40:21]. *See them standing all neatly in a row, the rather-bes. We are all one of them. We are all standing in our spaces we have created here in this plane we call* earth, *for the convenience of space then allows us to foremost move forward with our rather-bes. Rather-be is not entirely a place of discontent; it is simply a soul crying out for what it does best, which is create and change. Do not fear change; change is the impetus of all that is to come, and all that has been before, and will be. Change is the Christ that all your belated* [sic] *brethren are so fond of speaking for. Christ is change. To be "in Christ" is change. To bless Christ is change. To be blessed by the Savior Christ is change. I emphasize change because he is essentially forever following this change process from the moment he appeared in your time, and* [even] *before that from the eternity from whence he sprang. So this Christ which* [who] *was crucified, was not just the guidance to goodness only but the willingness, the willingness forever to change. The flexibility to change. How many times must I say this word? It is so that you may know that all you have felt sad for the past few days, these changes you have mourned, are not endings as you have mourned them. They are beginnings to new realities that you are forming now as I speak. They are freedom to yet another, yet a new way.*

Simeon's way of describing the human evolutionary or expansion principle as *rather-bes,* to me is very apt for our twenty-first century western thought. At least a few religious persuasions scold followers for even mild discontentment, while I believe Simeon attempts in the previous paragraphs to engender a different understanding about the human hankering to explore new possibilities within the realm of change. "Rather-be" can be as much a creative process as "being."

A few days prior to receiving this session, I'd felt the weight of changes that come with aging and losing the ones we love. I'd lost my maternal grandmother a few years back and was particularly recalling some of the finer details of her life just the week before: the way she rolled out homemade pie crusts, or the sound of her laughter.

These proponents of change occur as we observe change about us. I believe Simeon refers here to the most fundamental change of all reality: the change that lies in the eye of the observer, particularly when a person decides to accept life through a higher state of consciousness that is available to everyone.

When Simeon announces, *"We are one in the same . . ."* is he announcing himself as the Biblical Simon Peter? On the outset, it appears so. But later in this chapter and throughout the book, Simeon repeatedly emphasizes the reality of the oneness of all and our illusion of seeing ourselves as separate beings. In that construct, he claims oneness with all things.

Simeon explains about his parenthetical statement *I will show you a greater reality in just a moment* later in a session on July 31.

ALMOST TWENTY QUESTIONS

I wasn't sure about posing direct questions to Simeon just yet. Maybe it's too early, I thought. Besides, I had so many questions; it was difficult to narrow it down to just a few. But these are seven I decided upon, following with his responses:

1. Could it be possible that I am only repeating here what I have read recently?

You'll see the difference as we go along. I will speak of more things.

2. Will you assist me as I am learning medical Qigong healing to do things that help others heal? (I'd had an interesting experience treating a client earlier that morning: it felt like someone else had placed a hand over mine.) Was that you this morning?

I'm closer than you think. Rest a minute. (I took a short break.) Then: *You're hiding around an informal way of conjugation. Let me be brief and clear: Give up the stipends when you can. You must earn four million the way you are headed, before I can tack your service. Do you see?*

I'm guessing that Peter, ever the fisherman, might be using this word *tack*, which can mean to change a course of action, as if pitching the sails on a boat to change direction. Regarding the stipends, I believe Simeon was addressing a bit of early defensive posture I was still clinging to, or my incessant and mercurial need for validation.

I remember telling my husband one time that I wished I had more incontrovertible proof regarding the paranormal. The problem is, a skeptic's proof is never enough. I could easily see how, with *that* kind of attitude, a person could bring home a seven-figure salary and still question his own financial success. The problem becomes a person's mental projection of what he values as supplying his individual worth, which, in this case, is far more transient than the individual's soul worth—his true worth. The answer to question two above, therefore, addresses the proverbial human dilemma that "enough is never enough."

3. I don't understand fully. How do I see?

It's a short time before you will be able to hear me clearly.

4. What about all these "almost" conversations going on in my head? The ones I can't really hear? Is that you, me, one, or many?

That is all the creative potential you are hearing. All the creative potential we have to offer you.

5. Do these voices involve some undeveloped personality or psyche of my own or others?

It's merely a wavelength of potential. Nothing to fear.

Thank you, Simeon.

This will fall nicely over time.

6. How will you greet me? How will I know your presence? (I saw here several symbols—a TV screen, a necklace, and a flower. I found myself unable to settle on the start of a sentence.) Then:

It's the same as all others [symbols]. I could use the image of a TV screen, a necklace, a flower—but I will choose to touch you on the shoulder.

7. How will that feel then?

This will pull your hair just slightly.

At the time, the entire session just—took off. I still struggled to believe I'd one day hear Simeon more clearly or that he would produce enough material to have a book. That night I decided I'd just have to run with what I had taken down and leave it at that. In my own strange way, that was my beginning of trust. I would continue the same process the next night, and the night after that.

The following morning, I took the time to reread the two epistles of Peter.

JULY 26

After last session's apparent success, I come tonight with trepidation, harboring the fear of not receiving the same, or having beginner's disappointment after beginner's luck. Of course, I still have many, many questions, but I'm unsure when or how to ask them. Shortly before I came out to the cabin, I experienced a thick feeling gathering around the right side of my face. I have no idea what this pulling of the hair will feel like; perhaps it is even the band of vibration I felt last night.

UNIVERSAL CRUCIFIXION

Simeon indicated for me to move (my chair) up a little, and that he'd be *right over*. I did, and I noticed that the band was back, and fairly strong, almost tickling.

Therefore, since you are being so very careful concerning that which you think you receive, the plan must be altered a bit until you give over your fear and stronghold. Perhaps thoughts of a different course will suffice to make you less tender around your high expectations.

Reporting: The past habit of mine to expound greatly concerning the meaning of a single word such as change *follows a range of thought and feeling. You see, behind every word comes a variety of possible evocative associations, and it is with those associations that man often finds himself gone awry. Suddenly, the world of his thought range takes upon itself an entire new meaning, that not far afield from a transmigration of identity that he did not heretofore perceive or understand. And so, as you troubled yourself today to scan the two epistles I am partly responsible for, I will offer some notes.*

The second coming of anyone or anything from its original form, the reincarnation of this life form, so to speak, is a remarkable event in and of itself. And so [is] the third, fourth, and fifth coming. It might seem strange that I trouble myself in the second epistle with the second, and merely the second, coming of Christ. Why not the third, fourth, or fifth? Why stop at the first reincarnation only, and focus on that? [sic] It is for that, and in the same reason, that I ranted so vividly about change—and was not quick to let it go, you see. For some, if not many, will never get past the idea or acceptance of a second coming, and what it truly represents. For if the Christ could not have come a second time, then his first time would've truly been for naught, and we, sad clones of his nonexistence. But he truly lives, as we will continue to live, long after our bodies have passed our own crucifixions—for you see, the process on that tree is not so different from the process of death in any other way, no matter how peaceful it may seem. So a woman who dies in her sleep "peacefully," by your terms, has still been crucified many times over, when we are considering the process of swiping [sic] her from this dimension to another.

And I know that you are awaiting the energetic explanation of crucifixion, and what matters we are concerned with: blood, air, and water exchange. These are possibly too complicated for you to fathom. But trust me—the process chemically, energetically—is of note, in that this continues to happen each time a body dies—exactly of that which the Christ experienced. Further inroads in science will eventually bear out this fact: that to suffer death is not to suffer in the context of how you have known it before. It is a transition that we may refer to as the universal crucifixion. The energy of the cross symbol is central in this scientific discovery and explanation.

And seeing how I have belabored that point, it is now necessary to return to my former emphasis on the Second Coming of Christ—for you see, there are many who have not gotten past this transition successfully in their hearts and minds even yet. If in context, we might consider that many saw him in reincarnate form; however, he was not returning at that moment to the womb. You have it clear. There are those who speak of the Christ as living in obscurity following that day on Golgotha, that it was not he who hung on the tree. They question rightly. The information was sketchy regarding just how he escaped and if he escaped. The doctrines that followed, including that of my own, had to account for his presence. (It is embarrassing to admit that we possibly lost him after following so closely those years.)

At the Second Coming, which I spoke for, the various and sundry explanations still rumble through the minds of the ever-questioning, and rightfully so. History has a way of obscuring the obvious. I did not know the man, the criminal, taken to be crucified. Period. This much is correct. The Jesus who rose again is the one for which I speak for in the Second Coming, and you must know that several years intervened that are not spoken for. The real Jesus may have died in obscurity as every bit as much in that he was born, and we saw him reincarnate before our eyes, the real flesh and blood, a living proof that we ourselves would follow in such a manner. But that was only his second [incarnation]. *With that, I ended my speakership. Let me remind you: These things are difficult to speak of. You should tread lightly. Do not be tortured by these explorations you are taking. Some will alter as we go, as the way becomes clearer to you. After all, your psyche is still under construction, my friend. The canon you read of me lately, save it for another time.*

Friends and colleagues alike have asked me whether Simeon is addressing the Biblical birth of Jesus as the very first incarnation, and if this would be appropriate from a reincarnation stance. From the context, he appears to be doing just that. However, Simeon's major focus seems to be about clarifying that he is speaking of reincarnation when he speaks of Christ's Second Coming, and *that* has been misinterpreted in Scripture as Christ's final appearance on earth.

Simeon's anachronistic use of *swipe*, a slang word for theft, doesn't seem to fit into his formal and archaic vernacular as an appropriate figure of speech, unless the death process is seen as a stealing away of the soul from the body. When one considers the myriad defense mechanisms and survival mechanics of the ego that keep the soul bound to the body, then this very well may serve as apt simile for death. Perhaps the process of card swiping for identification, authentication, or payment might serve as a metaphor here, as well.

It seems to me that a sentient being standing outside of the time-space continuum would naturally use archaic, anachronistic, as well as futuristic terms, so I am not surprised by odd word usage and what appear to be manufactured words from time to time in Simeon's discourse.

At first blush, Simeon's banter about " . . . *a woman who dies in her sleep peacefully . . . being crucified many times over"* seems ominous, at least until he dispenses the material in the following session (July 27) describing crucifixion as an energetic process that is universal to earthbound human beings during death.

These things, to be sure, were difficult for me to transcribe. Simeon's words went against every engrained belief system I had garnered since a very early age. Tread lightly, indeed. I was painfully aware that the entire foundation of conservative Christian theology requires a Messianic Savior to die on a cross, and its doctrines concerning the need for humanity's deliverance from sin requires Jesus' crucifixion remain historical fact. To remove him from such a position in history begs explanation.

It occurred to me later, as I researched some of the alternative theories about Christ, that this process was probably necessary for my growth and responsibility as a spiritual seeker. I'd always unquestioningly accepted that the historicity of Christ had transpired the way early church records had presented him to us. Was this really a responsible view?

What Simeon treads upon above is a body switch theory, which is recorded in an apocryphal Gnostic dissertation, *The Second Treatise of the Great Seth*:

"For my death which they think happened, happened to them in their error and blindness . . . it was not I. It was another, Simon, who bore the cross on his shoulder . . ."

These and other writings like those by Balisades from Alexandria during AD 120–130 and the Koran (4:157) centuries later record that Simeon of Cyrene was nailed to the cross in Jesus' place.

Another body switch theory promoted by the Mandaeans (a race of people originally known as Nasurai from southern Iraq and Iran) asserts that Thomas, called Didymos (the twin)—and possibly Jesus' biological twin, was crucified instead.

Other instances in the Bible indicate that Jesus was capable of and used invisibility techniques. On at least three separate occasions he was recorded as "passing through their midst," thus evading capture and death at those times (Luke 4:28–30, John 8:58–59, John 10:39).

This capability might be attributed to master escape techniques like that of the Sicarri or other invisibility and cloaking techniques. Many other written records exist that describe adepts and avatars who have harnessed the ability to make themselves momentarily invisible. In the Hindu doctrines of the Upanishads, supernatural powers called Siddhas are viewed as the natural outcome of mastery over one's mind and environment through serious study of raja yoga. One of the benchmark Siddhas is invisibility. Indian author and scholar Patanjali's ancient documents, the Yoga Sutras, describe men becoming imperceptible to other men through meditation and concentration. Patanjali explains that ". . . a direct contact with the light of the eyes no longer existing, the body disappears."

Just how invisibility works has been more recently released from findings of scientists at the University of California, Berkeley. Since we see objects when light reflects and scatters off them, invisibility techniques must employ negative refractive properties that keep light from being absorbed by or reflected off an object.

Another adept with similarly recorded abilities is the patriarch Moses. In *Antiquities of the Jews,* author Flavius Josephus wrote, "Now as he [Moses] went thence to the place where he was to vanish out of their sight, they all followed after him weeping; but Moses beckoned with his hand . . . and as he was going to embrace Eleazar and Joshua, and was still discoursing with them, a cloud stood over him on the sudden, and he disappeared . . ."

One modern record of invisibility was the case of Marie Harlowe in 1925. Harlowe, who worked in an industrial office, boarded a train for an appointment in a nearby town shortly after a disagreement with a local jeweler about the price of a ring. Harlowe, a student of Tibetan yoga, attributed what followed to her training. She later said that after she boarded the train, the conductor, jeweler, and sheriff entered the car where she sat. The jeweler had accused Harlowe of theft, and the three men walked down the aisle looking for her. They stopped where she was sitting, but seemed unable to see her. After a brief search, they disembarked to hunt for her in the train station.

I've included only some of the information I found concerning the possibility of Jesus' escape by invisibility. Simeon will speak later about nanoscale constructs of invisibility, shapeshifting, and cloaking in Chapter 11.

Given the nature of Simeon's material in the July 26 session, I originally thought about striking these words altogether. But after much consideration, I decided to let them stand. I felt certain that, at some point, we would revisit this subject of the life of Christ and crucifixion. Did Jesus really avoid crucifixion, and if in doing so, what was he intending to teach his followers? I made the commitment then to continue this venue on the possibility that Simeon would deliver this information later, and I decided to set aside my preconceptions long enough to allow this to happen. If I got it all wrong somehow, I trusted I'd be corrected.

Meanwhile time very much seems to march forward, and I've been invited to give the invocation at a medical banquet. What better source than Simeon? So I asked him for a prayer:

Let us pray:

> *May Heaven and earth stand before us*
> *today as we offer our heartfelt thanks for*

*the men and women who spare the lives
of those less privileged in health. All
healing springs from the Source of life
from which it came, our Maker, the
Alpha and the Omega* [Revelation 1:8
NIV], *the One who stands outside time as
we know it.*

*Thank Him accordingly each day for the
opportunity you have to cast your
shadow of love and health on those who
pass your way. For they are never alone
when love casts its comfort, its wisdom,
its life-giving force. Be not afraid, in all
that you do, and you will be already
blessed indeed. Amen.*

SAVE HERE

JULY 27

I'm sitting for a session earlier tonight. The two previous
sessions began around 9:00 p.m. and lasted until 10:15 p.m. Tonight I
am starting induction at 8:40 p.m.

As I walked out to the cabin, I noticed it is nearly a full moon,
and it seemed the moon had suddenly burst into fullness, considering
the significantly smaller size of the waxing gibbous phase the previous
night.

Although I have no agenda or idea what Simeon could possibly say, this is no different than the past two nights. As I go on this exploration or journey, I seem to be continually stumbling across different ways and means of communicating with this entirely sentient being.

Again, I received an indication to move over slightly to the right, which I did. I have a very subtle feeling that the left side of my face has flattened out, including the left eye, and this side of my face feels like it is hanging much longer than the right.

Tonight we will move forward with a few specifics concerning the notes of late. I would remind you that there is a certain quality to your life notes as you walk this earth, a density that each man or woman maps through the corridors of time. In its finality, these notes are the roadmap of many souls alike, crucifixion being the central theme. Obviously, not all men or women are physically crucified.

You may ask why such a grotesque form of symbol would carry itself through the centuries, the millennia, the corridors of time and become that which is common to mankind. I have said that the cross symbol, it is the evaporative process of the DNA helix spread over the time that it takes the soul to transmigrate from the body after death. In this transmigration, the soul shoots from the hip, so to speak, a directional flow not too unlike a crossbow, and the ethereal body is flung from its attachment to the midstream. [This description could be a nautical or even energetic term, implying the body's midline, Taiji Pole, or conception vessel as used in Traditional Chinese Medicine.] *In such a state, a soul may find itself scurrying back to the body, uncertain of what it has become. This cross shape is the code for transmigration, and the only code used thus far for humankind.*

Different entities use other symbols when speaking of death, but ours is the crucifix. The very shape of the body allows for an easy understanding of such a cross, lends itself to such a cross, although the physical usage for torture and punishment was a sorry creation of mass greed and barbarism. Christ crucified, as I have spoken of him, was content to say, a helpful illustration of what all men must find as they come unto death (this thrusting out and away from the body), the tent left behind.

Life yields such lessons unkindly, perhaps, but only for the creative purposes of the human soul experience. Without such experience, you would be parched indeed. The God I know saw to it that all creatures receive their chances to grow, learn, and transmigrate many times—yet find themselves with an endless variety of possibilities still. Therefore, eternity. Therefore, clocking the time from start to finish is only a convenience from era to era while the soul subsists within time as you know it. But this is a repetition for you. Should I go on? Save here. [Working in this small cabin without a battery backup was risky; Simeon seemed to be aware that I should save often during his discourse.]

The hope that we have here on this earth is a guarded and foolish one, by comparison with dimensions all around. As I have said, I travel over from my plane to meet you, and with this, I bring signals which fall into conceptual focus for forming words. In the Hebrew, sayonara [a Japanese word for good-bye, 19ᵗʰ century root translation "if it must be so"] *could mean something entirely different other than "peace be with you,"* [Hebrew *shalom*] *with rapid-fire* [sic] *molecules sending these words your way.*

When Simeon speaks about multiple transmigrations (reincarnations) as being *a repetition for you*, I believe he is referring to my own personal investigations regarding the plausibility of reincarnation. I think this is his way of saying he is not interested in making an apologetic case for reincarnation at this point.

I was a little mystified by Simeon's directive to *save here*, particularly since he did not continue much longer with that session. As it turns out, I was unaware that my laptop's battery and power source were rapidly deteriorating underneath me. The recovery of a session later lost in September due to simultaneous battery and power cord failure was an interesting event in itself. Simeon, apparently an ancient entity, seems not only to have a window to understanding modern technology, but also a precognitive one, at that.

Another anachronistic usage is found when the term *rapid-fire* is thrown into a riddle Simeon presents at the end, possibly directed toward assuaging my concerns with getting this right. (I would avoid at all costs using words like *rapid-fire* as descriptive choices in my own writing.) And the molecular difference between *sayonara* and *shalom*?

How many of us consider the molecular construct of words? How many of us consider the ultimate molecular effect of choosing one word over the other? Does their molecular contruct really count in our everyday banter?

THE NATURE OF TIME AND SPACE

JULY 30

I found the following quote afterward, which seemed a fitting summary of the upcoming session:

"People like us, who believe in physics, know that the distinction between past, present, and future is only a stubbornly persistent illusion."

—Albert Einstein

To contemplate the future is the pulse of eternity, one beat at time. As it seems this way, we are stretching a series of beats drumming through our veins from one to the next, while we are here in this body. [I was extremely aware of my pulse on the back of my neck, particularly the low cervical spine, an experience I've never felt before, not even during athletic endurance trials.]

All course of life and breath, health and death, are coursing in and couched in this thing we call time. If I were to tell you that time runs backward, in essence, you would find it hard to believe or grasp the concept, as you have been told many times before, that time's essence is free of itself, quite literally—you may traverse in the yesteryears of your soul as easily as you may move forward in this plane to another course of action.

Should I say that if time indeed runs backward as simultaneously as it can run forward, you see, this disembarks you into an entirely new dimension and journey altogether. It is not steep or thin, short or small, either—for space cannot capture what it is [means] *to exist. Space is one of the means whereby we describe our existences, to be sure. This traverse in time has yet to be understood by greater minds in the future/past, you see, for they are one in the same. Until you stand outside of it* [space or time], *you cannot understand it.*

The previous session marks the first of Simeon's repeated discourses concerning the nature of time and space, and his assertions appear to fall in line with quantum theory. When quantum theorists chase down the nature of an atom, the stuff of which solid matter—you, me, the table—are constructed, they discover that an atom contains 99.9 percent empty space. That's because atoms are made of energy that is bound into fluctuating, immaterial fields, and the nature of solid matter is therefore more of an energetic process than it is an object. When we redefine matter as empty, fluctuating space, matter takes on an entirely different meaning, and what we have previously considered as "real for being solid" is no longer so. Three-dimensional matter becomes an illusion. The illusion of matter exists as solid because we, the observers, perceive this energy in an organized, solid energetic state.

By the same token, time in its observable state becomes nothing more than a mental construct, or a field of ideas. The reality of the concept "always now" or of empty space have no need for time or mass as directives. While time seems to occur in a chronological order, the theories of fluctuating, yet observable fields present to us something altogether different—the possibility of a journey only appearing to occur, and the simultaneous ability to stand outside that journey in a completely different reality called "always now," or non-time. If anything, the journey we think we're on never occurred, and a greater reality involves the removal of both concepts: time and space. No journey—only awakening to an awareness of non-journey.

These alternative thoughts about time and space are difficult to grasp, let alone accept. The human ego seeks to preserve itself and what it perceives as its own survival insurance by keeping the time continuum alive. The ego needs the continuity of bringing the past along to the present. It understands the present and arranges the future in terms with the past. Thus, even while we may live in time only as a mental construct, we continue to arrange events chronologically and meet our past over and over again.

Time running backward? Enter Dean I. Radin, D.J. Bierman, E.C. May, and their published research on time-reversed human experience, precognition, and human consciousness. Hundreds of papers like these about time-reversal phenomena are available in both physics and philosophical literature.

For example, researchers Levin & Kennedy (1975) used a reaction time task to see whether contingent negative variation (a slow brainwave indicator of anticipation) might be used to unconsciously detect a stimulus that would randomly appear in the future. Test participants were asked to press a key when a green light appeared, but not a red light. An electronic random number generator would select which light would appear. Levin & Kennedy observed significantly larger contingent negative variation (slow brainwave activity) just before the random number generator selected a green light, but not a red light.

These and other studies indicate there are built-in precognitive abilities in human consciousness—with implications from a certain number of staged trials that information in the future can indeed also flow backward in time. Perhaps this accounts for some of the strange occurrences and space-time distortions to linear time that some people experience during perceived life-threatening events or crises.

Shortly before finishing the manuscript, I received another insight regarding this space-time reality Simeon is referencing. The basic message was, "Look behind you in time for all that you ask; it is already yours." It occurred to me that when Jesus spoke about asking with a faith that you have already received (Mark 11:24 NIV), this was more than just a qualifier for the kind of belief a person would exercise.

Jesus was calling his followers to align themselves with quantum reality, to regard their prayer requests in light of quantum reality. It's more than just behaving as if, or feeling joy that, one's prayers are already answered, though that's certainly a big part of the equation.

The recipe for quantum prayer is this: glance over your shoulder, behind you, as if looking into your past—and there, your future needs are already answered—for time as you understand it does not exist. Don't get me wrong—when using our physical senses, we still experience things linearly, and it does appear that personal needs arise consecutively along a time-space continuum. But I think we are being called to view time in this new way, inside a quantum reality.

Simeon says our needs were never separate as we see them, view them, or pray for them. They are all synchronized: already answered, accomplished, and completed.

GUILT AND SUFFERING

JULY 31

A paradigm of all that is complete is the Maker of the event: you or another, or en masse in time. The focus of every event in time is thrust upon you without mercy, in a sense—for in this time, you are acting accordingly to that which you believe to be true. Hence, even your belief that time exists binds you in such a way to itself and becomes paramount to the other funneling of belief systems that pour without.

Tantamount to your understanding of time and its importance or unimportance to you in any given existence is your understanding of where you have been, or your origins. Therefore we will digress a bit from this discussion concerning time to that which hence originates all energy and matter. The fulfillment of All That Is in energetic form is here and now, and always in the here and now. It is not somewhere far removed from your own person at any given moment. Thus, the supreme importance of understanding the now, [or] the eternal *moment—that does not exist in time. You may experience it often while you channel on this earth, for you see, that is what each and every human being is up to—channeling his or her energy in human form, in this physical body, here in time. You are not far from hearing me now. My voice is unlike any you have ever heard, although you have heard one like it. Order is paramount in this project. You and June* will find the way. That is a given.*

Parallel to all that lies underneath your coming in this lifetime, or anyone's coming in this lifetime, is that which all of mankind must suffer and enjoy. Suffering comes before the deluge of mankind will hope to see what is left to enjoy. The nature of suffering is to put it out of one's way, to make sure that it is no longer an issue for the next generation of one's soul. For the soul must on the outset delude itself that suffering is a necessary part of existence, even while roaming here on this cursed earth with its [seeming] *fragments of humanity and goodness. For you see, suffering is no more than a mass delusion of all mankind, and it is no more necessary than the next one would have it be. Nature does not suffer in the same way you do, in consciousness. It seeks its own destruction at times, but in this destruction, it is not plagued with the guilt for its very existence and its actions in time, as you are.*

It is this guilt we must address. For in guilt, all of mankind winds down to nothingness, and in this nothingness, he finds himself at last. The guilt is not there. It is superimposed upon a man's heart like a

---

* June Ford was my friend and editor for several writing projects, and especially helpful in organizing Simeon's material.

painting, like a wild 3-D image, if you will. A wildcard it is. It is no more necessary that man find in his fright that he was cast out from unity with God. The reason that the feelings persist so well is because they are ingrained from birth—not mere social conditioning, you see, but truly ingrained in our fiber as we must leave other domains to find birth in this one. It is hence a type of separation that is unfathomable in the other earths, or palaces, where the souls of energy continue to exist after "death" in this plane. Hence suffering is for the weenies [sic] *that have nothing better to do with time than to find a way out of it.* [At this point, I protested that I thought using the term *weenies* was rude.] *You may use downtrodden instead of weenies, if you must. Suffering isn't courageous, even if it takes much chutzpa to force such an existence upon oneself. Suffering is simply not necessary. It is a well-encoded belief system, interlaced in the human DNA from birth. The viewpoints and belief systems men adopt* [will] *enhance, replenish, or diminish suffering accordingly. This you must know and describe for those who believe they suffer. "Suffer no more! Christ has come!" This has been said, that he took our stripes for us* [Isaiah 53:5]. *What this means is, he buried the very encoding of suffering with his own birth and death. He made it necessary for us to look upon him, his life, and how he handles this concept of suffering, even that upon a cross. My word to you is he avoided it. Suffer not the little children. Do not teach them that they must suffer. Life on the earth brings what one believes. Suffering will surely be a part of it, but even in these moments, there is the encoding the power within your energetic systems to undo that suffering. You should focus only on that.*

Time is an illusion. You have known this well. With time, mankind must suffer in those moments he chooses to make the moments of suffering, you see. With that suffering, he will learn that in essence, he must transcend time to relieve himself of it. He must focus merely on the moment in which he might improve his suffering lot and then again, and again, until he has a string of moments, a twine wire, so to speak, a line or continuum of nonsuffering moments. It is really that simple.

"Outrage!" I can hear the people already. "Heresy!" But in this time, you see, if he [mankind] *should transcend it, so that it no longer exists for him, he has ultimate control of all that found itself in that moment. And suffering no longer exists. This was the element, the secret, if you will, that saw many of us through martyrdom and death.*

In the streets where Jesus frequented with the "tax gatherers and sinners" [Matthew 9:11 NIV]*, there were many who laid aside their wares and followed him to the next town, far more* [instances] *than recorded. He garnered mass followings, speaking often as he went along, shouting through the streets what he felt in his heart at the moment, for the condition of mankind. For there in those streets he saw people hanging onto their suffering like a belt of foal. (You can look that up. It was popular in those days.) He wanted them to know that it was no longer necessary, at any rate, to live with their plight. The power to change was always theirs, even those structures in their existence that seemed the most unchangeable. The forgotten wares were often consumed and exchanged by the moneychangers at the temple (where he is so famous for his vile language). They truly were thieves looking for prey. And they, most of all, did not understand his* *words on how to end their own suffering. They saw no reason to end what they did not understand.*

A GREATER REALITY

Why did you choose crucifixion upside down?

Perhaps it would be easier to explain to you why I did not choose to die another way. To be fed to the lions, or to have one's life taken in a gladiatorial event, was a cruel and unusual punishment indeed. The souls who submitted to them were often parched beyond their ability to even walk, starved beyond the ability to stand. They were easy prey, and the events themselves lasted longer because of the circus surrounding them, the audience's pleasure.

I had no desire to die in a circus. I was willing to be martyred as my lord was scheduled to be, then eluded, as I have spoken, for I would choose to undergo that form of punishment later in life, for it had a certain measure of control and solitude. It was reserved for the most vile of offenders still, and its somewhat stationary measure allowed me the quietude to focus my mind out of time, and therefore [out of] suffering, to the death. When Job became the richest man who ever lived, following his great suffering, he would ne'er resist the moment to offer peace to his soul for all that he had lost, in order to learn how to live in the moment—the empty moment in time—beyond time.

I was set to continue, but I heard my son knocking on the door.

I came back a few minutes later, but my mercurial self was again working overtime. I decided to address Simeon with some of my own personal concerns:

I still feel as if I'm not receiving any of this from you. It's like it is being sifted through a filter in my brain. I'm not engaging in a deep enough trance, or what I deem as a deep enough trance, to hear you, either—I'm merely following hunches of words.

Your thoughts are my thoughts. Be not afraid or worried that we cannot correct much of this together at a later date, if we find it even necessary. You can read it back to me in your mind and ask me to comment. That is what I meant about order. Do not be disturbed by your alertness. This will come and go over time. If you wish me to speak through you, that can happen as well. It is not a place very far from where you are now. You simply need to be receptive to whatever thought comes your way. Trials come and go. You must settle on something that serves you best in order to communicate more fully with me.

Dreams will filter through to you about what you must know in order to communicate more effectively with me and through me. Remember that your concepts of space and time do not apply. You must accept this in order to continue without driving yourself nuts. The plus is: you are willing, at least thus far, to allow me to communicate through you this way. In the morning, you often are amazed by the way the words have come through so evenly and quickly. It is not that you could not write this all yourself, but you would not find any reason to, and you would pore over it for greater words here and there which I do not offer. That is the writer in you, my friend.

Take heart. The class is not far. More later on that.

What about the greater reality you told me you would show me in a moment in the session on July 23?

The reality, which I said I would show you, happened the moment your hands touched the keys. You do not remember, but the vibrations you felt were of such that you felt in charge, that what you were taking was of some import, you see. This greater reality is all that exists outside of time as you know it. There are energy vibrations that take on so many forms, and in their weaker and lesser moments, no form is necessary. This is lesser by your earth terms. Not necessarily elsewhere would this [the terms lesser or weaker] *have the same meaning at all.*

The import, which you have in doing this, is one that will follow you the rest of this life. Do not forget that.

Thank you.

You're welcome. You will wait for another night, and then we will continue on this path. My goodbye for you tonight is: betwixt and between. If this has meaning, so be it.

I always sensed that Simeon was very patient and gracious with me during the time I adjusted the way I received clairaudient information and decided upon what I was willing to trust. I was used to receiving audible perceptions of voices, tones, or noises; therefore, receiving material by mental impressions was still something very new to me. I tried another experiment. As I retired at night, I would ask for a few words from Simeon. In the hypnagogic state I would receive a perfect admixture of both. A mental impression would start a sentence, and every third or fourth word would come forward audibly between the mental impressions. This was exciting because these experimental discourses with both audible and inaudible material wove together in a completely comprehensible way. I didn't record any of these experimental sessions because in every instance, merely a few minutes after receiving them, I could not recall anything that was said.

Simeon makes a valid argument when he says ". . . *you would pore over it for greater words here and there which I do not offer."* Much of his repetitive word usage and manufactured words would have long ago been victim to my thesaurus, if these sessions were coming solely from me. Lack of word variance and word manufacture are pet peeves of mine.

In Buddhism and Hinduism, followers are taught to set aside the suffering, egoistic self and immerse themselves in the emptiness of All That Is, therefore allowing the Higher Self to emerge and be. Though life and its lessons appear to unfold in chronological order, these teachings beckon followers to the discovery of peace, nirvana, or perfection by learning to live in the present, or *eternal moment.* This is a way of burying the encoding of suffering and transcending time.

Given the bustling transcontinental trade during the time of Christ, it is plausible that Jesus could have traveled east during his "missing years" to study eastern religion. Ancient Buddhist volumes found at the Hemis Monastery in the 1800s present scattered accounts of a man named Issa (Jesus in Greek) who joined a trade caravan to the Far East at the age of thirteen. Enough similarities exist between Christ's (recorded) spiritual outlook and the teachings of Indian prince Siddhartha Gautama, or Buddha (*c.* 560 BC), to cause some to wonder if Christ found much of his inspiration in Buddhism. At the time of Jesus' life, it was not at all uncommon to take religious pilgrimages to India or the Far East—spiritual quests to incorporate the teachings of Hinduism, Buddhism, or Jainism. Similarities also exist between the teachings of Christ and Chinese philosopher Lao Tzu (*c.* 500 BC). Jesus is quoted, "Blessed are the meek, for they shall inherit the earth" (Matthew 5:5). And Lao Tzu: "Heaven arms with gentleness those it would not see destroyed." [*Tao Te Ching* 67] The aim to transcend suffering as Simeon described above is inherent in each of these eastern religions.

Simeon also mentions above that nature provides an example in that it does not *suffer in consciousness* like we do. This is because nature does not experience itself as separated from its Source and therefore guilty in the way we do, although Simeon acknowledges that nature *seeks its own destruction at times.*

Also, Simeon touches upon the crucifixion principle lightly again, that Christ, in *burying the encoding of suffering* and by avoiding suffering, was attempting to teach his followers about the undoing of the concepts of suffering and separation. Whether or not Jesus truly escaped crucifixion, I think Simeon communicates an entirely different message that Jesus attempted to substantiate, but that his followers may have missed. Jesus' perhaps successful attempt to avoid crucifixion had more to do with communicating to his followers something new about time, space, and transcending both of them, which included transcending suffering. Jesus very well may have been demonstrating the nature of quantum reality.

In 1983, physicist John Wheeler set out to establish a variation of an earlier quantum theory experiment in 1979. Scientists in the earlier experiment had already successfully shown that a photon fired at a target somehow "knew" whether it would arrive as a single particle or a wave. If the photon traveled through one slit to the target, it remained a particle. If it traveled through two slits, it moved as a wave. The conclusion: the scientists influenced the way the photon behaved by their foreknowledge of how the photon would be sent. Wheeler tweaked the experiment, having the observers choose how the photon would arrive after it had passed the barrier, but before it reached the target. Repeated trials yielded the same results: though the observers were choosing the destination results after the experiment began, they were also changing the way the experiment began. Wheeler's conclusion was startling: the choices that we make next week may, in effect, influence what just happened to us five minutes ago.

Could this quantum idea be the springboard for transcending suffering, and the reason Simeon declares that Jesus sought to avoid it, that *there is the encoding, the power within your energetic systems, to undo that suffering?*

The closing statement, *"My goodbye for you tonight is: betwixt and between,"* is further delineated in a prayer Simeon quotes at the end of a session later, on August 19.

I purposely did not include notes at the front end of the next session as a way of putting Simeon to the test. I thought about this for some time, that I wouldn't blame Simeon if he didn't look upon that favorably, because to put anyone to the test is to operate out of mistrust.

But, after all, he said we would *". . . wait for another night, and then . . . continue on this path."* Here's what I did: I didn't review the previous session, as was my custom by now. I was really curious how Simeon would continue after my son's interruption. When I'd resumed that session that day, we'd moved away from the original session material to address my personal concerns.

Also, I'd asked for a dream that might enlighten me about the *"belt of foal"* after searching for its possible meaning on the Internet. I could not find any such word foal, fole, phole, or any other phonetic spelling or meaning of this word regarding early first century commerce, fabric, material, or wares of any sort. It also occurred to me that Simeon might be speaking of the phylactery belts worn by various priests of religious sects like the Sadducees and Pharisees. However, his comment that *"it was popular in those days"* threw me off a little, and seemed to negate this interpretation.

A couple of nights later I dreamt about a young, dark-headed man who I believe represented Simeon Peter showing me a book that had a series of index or library cards used as markers. It made me think that this "foal" might be suggesting some early form of codex or perhaps parchment or papyrus paper that would be sold in rolls or belts. I continued researching this word and decided to inquire of Simeon in an upcoming session should nothing turn up. (I would later find out that the dream held yet another interpretation.)

Chapter Three

Another Vortex

AUGUST 5

Our vacation this year marked some changes for me that I hadn't expected. Eureka Springs, Arkansas, is reputed as a spiritual vortex, rife with the mystique of Indian lore, healing springs, and haunted hotels. I've always felt quite endeared to Eureka Springs and excited about being there. The magic wasn't the same this year, albeit I enjoyed my stay.

This morning, I have some time alone to sit for Simeon. It will be my first attempt to contact him away from home, in our hotel room. We'll see if anything comes over, or if I should wait until this evening when I'm home again.

For anything to be certain, you must coordinate the functioning of the entire realm of [the] mind. It is not just the two hemispheres alone; for should they cease to function, one over the other, this happens altogether too frequently. This union of mind begins outside the body, it swirls around you and encases you like a shadow; it is the shadow with which I healed many. This shadow self will spring henceforth from the cavity outside the body, which is otherwise known as spirit. How can I say this? It is difficult. The shadow which you

*have, you see, this spirit that encases the body yet stands outside of it,
[is] connected only by foreign matter, so to speak, for it is an umbilicus
that will be finally discarded when the body no longer walks this plane.
It is foreign in that it has no recourse beyond this world which you
have made, and which you continue to make, with your thoughts.*

*To miscreate is to fathom that you, or I, or anyone else in this
wretched state on the earth might find our way out by bodily means. It
is not so. To miscreate does not make it so, although at times, it may
certainly appear to make it so. When you understand the full extent of
what miscreation will do, you will be able to chastise the flesh for its
participation in an event that truly has no place in the kingdom of God.
This chastisement is not punishment; I was misquoted and I miscreated
on this myself [1 Peter 2:11]. This chastisement is formed from the root
[word] "chastity" in Hebrew, that is, it means that one finds in the
flesh a unique symbol and reality for all that the flesh may have to
learn while it roams here on earth. The body is a learning device; it is
merely a tool for the mind to encroach its feelings and pleasures and
desires. In the end, however, the body will have learned the power of
every human mind, and their thought processes, you see. The mind will
encroach in the sense that it must sway the body by its power, one way
or the other, in hope for finding a way to express itself completely. This
is your creation and miscreation. The way to distinguish between the
two is [by] combining your data and determining what will truly last.
All on this earth will be scorched away. So that in the end, in new
earths and new planes, you will still find yourselves creating and
miscreating what will and will not last. What will last are all acts*

performed out of undefiled love, undefiled and encroached upon by egocentric desire for the body or its preservation beyond that which it is intended to serve. Bear this in mind always, and you will be blessed. Treat the body with kindness by construct; the construct of your very own thoughts. They [the thought processes] *will indeed suffer or destroy or uplift or deny or soil or spoil or divide or conquer, or any of the life events in which the body is used and involved. This is not the end of what we will say about the body, but sayonara for now.*

I found it interesting that the previous session occurred the morning after I'd listened to a discussion over lunch between two doctors about biochemical changes that occur in the left and right cerebral hemispheres during high-intensity endurance exercise. The "runner's high," an athlete's sense of serendipity or "performing in the zone" during endorphin reuptake, has been extensively researched, particularly its roles in cortical processing. Simeon makes no bones about it: thought processing occurs outside the cerebral hemispheres as well. Mental fields are potentially vastly larger than the human brain. When writing cover copy for this book, Simeon introduced:

There are mapped lines of tenure producing uninterrupted peace, love, and joy.

Thought, then, becomes property of spiritual essence, existing in thought forms, air speeds, and mapped structures outside of our bodies, invisible to the naked eye. Moreover, certain thought forms seem to contain or hold as longer-term "property value" those intangibles for which mankind longs: love, peace, and joy. We might go so far to say that our entire earth existence finds its meaning by recognizing one pattern after another or by connecting a series of patterns. This *mapping*, or patterning, gives us the structure and ability to recognize and experience love, peace, and joy. (Simeon has more to say concerning this subject in the following chapters.)

Regarding the *"healing shadow"* Simeon speaks of, historical records identify the Apostle Simon Peter as a healer as well as a canonized saint. Crowds would throng about, trying to stand in the apostle's shadow in order to be healed.

UNTIMELY DEATH

As I explained in the foreword, it's my nature to dive into personal interests with no holds barred, which always places me at a risk for burnout. I guess you could say that I went into the early sessions constantly measuring my gusto factor, well aware of my tendency to try too hard—which might inhibit this process altogether. I was always eager to hear what Simeon had to say, though much of the time I walked away with many more questions. Therefore, I rarely sat for more than one session a day. The session below is one of those rare occasions I sat for more than one session.

I'm back home again, and decided to sit for a second session this evening.

It is to honor oneself in this manner, to receive that which is [bit by bit] *foretelling in one sense, but also a more complete picture of one's entire psyche; the psychological journey in toto* [in total]. *For so many people will never completely allow themselves to come apart in this way; to stare their destinies in the face altogether and say, this is it! It is for this reason that we must depart the earth many times, the culminating point of these many, many destinies we will start and ne'er finish. If it were not this way you see, it is of the foremost reasoning that a man should "eat, drink, be merry; for tomorrow I may die"* [Isaiah 22:13, Luke 12:19]. *Thus directing one's life course in such a way is not altogether heretical, hedonist, or licentious in fashion; simply an acknowledgement that the course will be changed yet once again, when the soul is carried away in the bird's beak* [during death], *as people once were so fond of reasoning in superstition.*

The souls of children would not suffer long in their course, you see, if they knew ahead of time what it was like to become old. Many of them do [know]. *For it is merely a few of these children (in comparison to all who have lived in all times), who come to this plane full knowing (in their consciousness knowing that, but not in their physical brain) that they must die young. "Only the good die young" while on the one hand might stand for a misnomer, on the other states principle: the young fodder for the earth's sake may be harmed if their intentions lead them further into* [that] *life itself, further along the path toward aging and decay. The intention from the onset of such a short-lived version into adulthood is such that the individual, the soul, you see, has curtailed and curtained his or her life (however ignobly this may take place), and has chosen the means to avoid at that time another digression of the soul, another change, another spark of creativity, another outlet for expansion. To be sure, the soul that has crossed over will continue its expansion on the plane in which it finds itself next; however, the soul has in a sense shunned what earth may have had to offer at that time. The soul has cut short the learning curve by a few paltry years, or so it thinks, when quite another process has gone forth. The soul must learn in order to understand that if it must come again— although the shorter the better might seem the best recourse—the best policy the instruments with which the elements surrounding us have to teach—the instruments will recourse to their earlier state to accommodate the wandering soul, the psyche that has refused to grow and accommodate all that it can be. This refusal is like an endless Ping-Pong game after the fashion of playing to the first defeat—the first missed ball or play, so to speak. However, the soul that unifies with itself—its Creator, its created, and All That Is—this soul shall traverse the earth with less shortened spans, less unnecessary interruptions. This soul will speak for all mankind and shape the earth in a new way, the soul who speaks for unity with its brother, its mother, father, and sister—there are no ties this excludes. This union, the co-mingling of all matter and souls, is the necessary issue in all life, no matter how brief, how cut short, how replayed, how incomplete. The human psyche will over the course of time find itself, and when it has come to the realization of what it is, that there was no or little need to find anything, then the psyche will in one sense find its rest. For ye are completed in Him, the Source, after all.*

What were the belts of foal you mentioned session before last?

In the cities there were salesmen and women who thought the country was at times a better place for marketable farmed goods, and refused to come into the city streets. In these countryside cottages, the wares were often laid on belts of material called fole—*and fole was therefore also used in transport to and from the city. Fole was the innards of a lamb or sheep, the skin or parchment of the animal hide. The hides were tanned for endurance and wear. They were popular in that they protected the commodities going to and from. The reason that I mentioned these belts and their common usages was* [that] *for the average person who incorporated this belting of wares to and from the cities a sheep-borne disease was very frequent. This caused great razing of the tissues of the hands and feet and was the culprit of their great suffering. It spread throughout the cities at times in untold numbers.*

If the concept of playing to first defeat in a game of Ping-Pong applies to the first time a player misses returning the ball, this can occur rather suddenly among skilled and unskilled players alike. This would therefore be an apt illustration of untimely death. When Simeon puts forward *"only the good die young"* as a misnomer, I believe he is simply saying that any of our earthbound sayings, attempts to explain or soften untimely death, or our efforts to comfort the bereaved are posited in our own perceptual limitations.

If we view the journey of the psyche in light of reincarnation, these untimely deaths can take on the meanings that Simeon employs. Probably the most complex and difficult portion of the soul journey is the emotional journey of the psyche, and Simeon emphasizes that it's a slower journey, requiring many lifetimes. Esoteric teachings supporting reincarnation maintain that the soul makes a series of choices or contracts before incarnating, even choices about a life cut short. Growth of the psyche continues in earthbound and non-earthbound states. According to these teachings, the psyche grows more rapidly in the earthbound state. Consider, for example, the journey of one's psychological experience of, say, dialing a three-digit telephone number to "Central" in 1935 at age twenty, to a five-digit rotary telephone in 1970 at age fifty-five, to a nine-digit push-button cell phone number in 2000 at age eighty-five—and that's merely a handful of selfsame evolving psychological experiences in one lifetime. The session given on August 5, is a difficult one to interpret, but possibly asks one of the most important questions of all: Why don't we all live to a ripe old age? I don't think Simeon sees either event, dying old or dying young, as "good" or "bad." He simply states that the soul that lives a shortened lifespan will move on to other existences, halls of learning, and perhaps return to earth life at a later date, more committed to stay the course to an older age.

An interval of three weeks had transpired since Simeon's first mention of foal, and I'd been rather disappointed that my efforts to identify the term had turned up dry. When I took this session, I got the strong impression that "fole" was the clearest phonetic spelling for this ancient Middle-Eastern idea. One disease that can be transmitted from

from sheep to humans is cutaneous (skin) anthrax, caused by the bacteria *Bacillus anthracis*. It presents as a boil-like skin lesion that forms an ulcer with a black center, or eschar, about two weeks after infection. In its early stages, the skin blisters, itches, and significantly swells.

Latter-stage cutaneous anthrax is relatively painless to the skin's surface, however, because the lesion forms a necrotic ulcer. Left untreated, cutaneous anthrax can progress to toxemia accompanied by fever, headache, flu-like symptoms, and death, which probably occurred frequently in the early first century. For tanners today, exposure to hazardous chemicals in processing baths can cause skin rashes as well as irritation of the eyes and respiratory tract. On the International Hazard Datasheets, biological hazards are still listed for tanners, whose exposure to raw hides and skins may dispose them to leptospirosis, tetanus, Q-fever, brucellosis, or anthrax.

What was the dream about the book marked with library cards?

When you write it down, you mark my words for the book we are planning. You will be forced to mark and reorder a few times, like switching chapters here and there for better readership. It will be a book that will be checked out numerous times. A wide readership. But you will be forced to divide it into sections because of the nature of the content. After this, you will find that things come together nicely once again.

If you must go rest now, remember to be well.

Thank you.

MATRIX OF POTENTIAL

AUGUST 7

With training, you will come to see that in another form, you can find me. It is not as difficult as you would suppose it so. In fact, the form is before you at this very moment and not yet deciphered by your vibrational awareness. You are close; fear not. In moments in the past when you have warily looked over your shoulder expecting to be spooked upon any second, those are the moments where you have been more accessible for those who come over. We are the channelers into your dimension, so to speak, by attuning ourselves to your vibrations when they are necessary and ready. For you see, the outcasts of society are often found by us to make the focus where it needs to be in order to receive such thoughts of unbending nature. For it is within everyone's nature to bend and turn thoughts where they will, with circular thought or reasoning, except for the few who find themselves downtrodden by the society in which they live. In these few (the ones who are or often feel outcast no matter whether this be in actuality or not), these outcast ones are the harbingers of our words and thoughts. It is an integral part of the psyche at work in the few who can hear and impress upon what we have to say. Remember that it is always and only always your choosing of me, as it is my choosing of you. This may sound contradictory, but this is the life breath of all choosing—God's, man's, and otherwise. It is a circular choice or choosing, you see.

When Simeon declares, *"We are the channelers . . ."* I think he is simply attempting to further clarify and expand his own information about channeling, emphasizing that this type of communication is a two-way transmission, requiring certain personality types and efforts by human channels, as well as specific attunements to human energies by the disembodied spirits.

I think the apparent contradiction in the session above comes from subtle differences in the word meanings "circular reasoning" versus "unbending thought" versus "'circular choice." In the material that follows, Simeon further delineates what he possibly means about circular choice.

In the middle of the universe is a cloud of thought pattern that rests its course toward earth and other planets containing sentient beings. In this pattern are the faces of the universe, myriad faces and concoctions of thought, will, and event-making patterns that are forever yours to contend with, play with, remark upon, and otherwise. It is a pool, so to speak, that some might regard as a cesspool if they see only what they determine is bad *or* evil, *for the thought chasers become the thought, you see. It is truly in the eye of the beholder whether these patterns will follow their courses toward what he or she might amass as good or evil days of their lives. Follow the days of their lives from start to finish, and the concoctions will always and evermore be what they have perceived them to be—happy, wretched, soiled, spooked.* [These are] *the myriad emotions that we apply when we make our judgment calls, you see, for what* [single] *judgment can we truly make without emotional content? It cannot be done. Thought is interlaced with emotion, and emotion, with thought. Perception and judgment join the mix out of necessity while we roam this earth.*

In the previous session, Simeon moves still further away from the concept of thought originating solely within the human brain, pointing toward an intergalactic source of thought forms.

Try as one might, Simeon announces rather bluntly that it is impossible to make a non-emotional judgment. The thought process is too tightly interlaced with emotion, he says. Perhaps this provides another key to understanding why many spiritual teachers instruct us to refrain from judging others, when we consider the impact of our own emotions on our lives.

BROKENNESS AND POWER

Simeon' first public statement was read at an interfaith ordination ceremony at the end of August. When I sat for the following session, I had a feeling he was about to deliver something to be read at this ceremony, but as always, I had no idea going into this session why he chose this particular topic. I'm nearly always surprised.

Growth and power come through the love that springs from all living things. When we speak of power, any negative connotations or judgments that hearken forward in your minds—let them go. Power is a plus for any living creature when it is used appropriately to do the bidding of serving the planet and all that it contains in gratitude, with fortitude and hope. This hope which you obtain from your faith in Spirit, God, All That Is, the Nameless One, the Allah, the Om, the Alpha encircling the Omega—well, you see, this inception of all that sprang forth to be what is to be today sprang from the utmost power and love and hope that ever transcended from within Itself [Himself]. This utmost power burst forth, sprang forth to become all that lives and breathes and dies again, the multiple realities, the planets, the solar systems, the universes, and those places, which you have no name for, those beings which have no form. All That Is manifested in this same power which you now might even at first-glance have an opportunity to scorn, if it were not from the inception of all creation, the spark which sparked all life, the [state of] Being which never began and never ends. And so, use the power that comes your way wisely, not to lord over others, not to compare, not to specialize or segregate, but to loan each brother and sister your life and the elements thereof as they are needed, as they may be extended–for to give is to take, to bend is to break—to be broken is only to be transformed into a greater reality. He was broken for our transgressions, you see—this Jesus found within himself the power to break himself on a daily basis while he lived on earth, and this (like the connotations of power), does not mean a broken spirit or soul, or whatever cash nonsense one might put in the offering plate of necessity to break or suffer as the Christ did. When he broke himself, he would simply strike out in another direction in faith, hope, and love—merely looking for another soul or subset of souls, another piece of the universe to share the depths of his psyche in a union so great we can scarce understand such kindness and wholeness. The breaking thereof did not mete out punishment to his or any other soul, did not find anyone or anything guilty, unworthy, lacking, evil, or otherwise. Brokenness was not a judgmental word, as it has been used and canonized altogether too well. This brokenness, let me see if I can find the explanation and hand it over to you now through this spirit which fights for the power to place it upon the keys—this brokenness, this suppleness of the flesh and the spirit would allow the lines of thought, of matter, of all that is to have the flexibility *to bend—to ply— to be pliable, that is to sway into another kind of existence at will, should that existence be necessary to bring a brother or a sister along the path to becoming more whole. And so, the* miraculous *(as you call them) healings, the many times that Jesus defied all that we then understood regarding matter, you see—these feats were generated by this brokenness, this suppleness of the psyche that he was willing to experience. His was and is openness unparalleled in history. Open your minds as wide as you can possibly allow, and it will not touch Jesus' brokenness and suppleness. Therefore, be broken, be powerful. The paradox seems simply astounding, I know. But consider each together, and you will find release for your souls. Amen.*

Simeon uses a good sense of humor with quirky rhymes in this statement in order to make his point. One moment I was typing along, and the next, I was struggling to find my hands on the right row of computer keys, fearing I'd lost my placement. Simeon alludes to a very commonplace use of the word "power," yet appropriate here, and as a good teacher would, he uses this everyday example to make his point. I think Simeon calls us to remember, also, that ordinary human abilities when strung together by commitment over time can have enormous impact. *That's* power.

Simeon also transliterated the concept of *brokenness* to *flexibility*, which seems to speak of Jesus' nonresistance. Did Jesus follow a pathway of nonresistance? This would most likely place Jesus among the Essenes, a Jewish sect that was peace loving and ascetic. Most lived a simple, monastic existence. Flavius Josephus called them "ministers of peace."

Philo, a scholar and contemporary of Jesus, wrote about the Essenes: "The first thing about these people is that they live in villages and avoid the cities because of iniquities . . . and pursue such crafts as cooperate with peace . . . you could not find any person making weapons . . . not a single slave is to be found among them . . ."

On August 15, Simeon added to this concept:

Nonresistance is the fabric of all furnishings. Gravitate toward what unites all, hold fast one to another, and realize this is the fabric of love.

Combining Simeon's thoughts about nonresistance, I'm reminded of the old adage, "What we resist, persists." If Jesus taught anything, it was "What you believe, is." I think Simeon is saying that this same belief system underlies whatever one chooses to resist. The more I resist something, the more I believe in it, and vice versa. I actually strengthen what I resist by my belief in it, and it pushes back. Nonresistance, often characterized by the ego as weakness, is a "letting go" or "allowing." Simeon says nonresistance is ever as much a creator of its own fabric and its own reality. If I choose to merge with a situation instead of resisting it, I become part of the fabric of a potentially new situation, infusing the situation with a completely different set of parameters.

The above material was taken in one session, considerably longer than an average session. I sensed that Simeon wanted to go on, but I also sensed hesitation. I thanked him and asked, "Do you have more?"

There is always more. You cannot take it all in one evening. I could go on and on, and your mind will begin second-guessing over time. Rest is necessary; pauses are necessary, so that you gain a greater field of reference by living life as you know it in the here and now. Be well.

RESTRUCTURING OF MOSES

AUGUST 8

My son was sick today, so I saw one client and took the remainder of the day off from homeschooling. I'm still dragging a little myself following a cold virus, but wanted to sit tonight to see if anything would come through.

Envelopes can be monumental in making the lessons more complete. Envelopes are sessions without encasement; open in their own right. And so when you push the envelope, you open the windows of opportunity with this [kind of] flexibility. The monumental pathways come from monumental lines and monumental openness, period. Now, in the vacuum, you see, are wonderments not of this earth or time, or space; it is a void, a most precious void, [with] none of your negative connotations, but instead a space for all that has to be, for all that can be. In the beginning, the great void, the expanse of the heavens, the toil of the earth that was not yet formed, was bottomless space created first, the very concept, you see, of space—not outer space, but the very concept of space had to come first. Then the space was filled with objects, and so, the concepts of mass and velocity, and so on.

God created the creatable. You create, at times, the uncreatable. What am I saying, you ask? The uncreatable are again the miscreations of the part of you that fears and does not love. Some might call it the Lucifer, or the evil within, but I prefer to call it the uncreated, the part of you that never was. It is a charade that has beguiled mankind since his roots, since his beginning, so to speak. For in Heaven from whence we came we knew full well at our inception no such space for beguilement existed at that point, before our reincarnation on earth. It is a difficult position to maintain, this beguiled and beguiling, one that requires so much effort on your parts, and scarce the ability to continue along your way with such heavy burden upon your hearts. For He would have you spare your stripes and look full into His face without fear.

When the prophet Moses dared look upon Him [Exodus 33:18–23], *he saw no impact upon his intrepid soul structure, you see. He saw time pass before his eyes in a flash, and he returned below several years older by earth years. The effects were purely biological. His aura, to be sure, was expanded to accept His mighty creator's light and life breath* [Exodus 34:29]. *But he was not extended beyond that which his soul could bear. He did not wait to receive more, as he could have. This lesson for him in time, and concerning time, was vital to his understanding about how time can be transcended, you see. He was one of the earlier transcenders. He was one who experienced firsthand a rapid-fire* [sic] *aging concept, and felt it deep in his bones, what it means to accelerate time. This may sound negative, this rapid aging of Moses. But for him, and only him, it was the perfect proof of the God of his people. It was the only miracle that he was ready to accept at that time. And so they saw him return as a wizened old man* [Exodus 34:30].

To put it lightly, there is no time that transcends that which Moses learned about on that hill in his life, for he has set himself as the archetype, a willing servant in what he would experience that day. As Moses walked the mount and returned the wiser, this was so because of his momentary freedom from time. He knew then that God was real. You may think that to be a paltry concept for a man so vigilant in His [God's] *keep; however, this was the albatross about Moses' neck, his lifelong struggle to speak for a God who spoke but did not appear, a time frame of reality that he accepted as his own but had not realized, or made his own. After that day, he made it his own. He had ridden the wave of time forward in merely a few minutes, and he* [Moses] *saw*

[knew] *everyday in his face what God could do and had done.*

I believe Simeon is pointing back to part of two very early sessions taken on June 15 and June 20, in order to clarify. In those sessions he indicated, *"Monumental lessons will happen along directly open pathways,"* and *"There needs to be a vacuum, and so for you to continue."* He continues to use anachronisms in the previous session and the next session, as well.

I questioned afterward why Simeon spent time talking about Moses. I think the key is Moses' relationship to time. After introducing Moses as an example of a time transcender, Simeon continues speaking about transcending time throughout his discourses.

The Biblical Moses has been identified in several texts as an ancient magician or wizard. Following some of the recorded feats Moses performed, we'd expect that he'd have no trouble believing the supernatural. But apparently, he did. Simeon notes that Moses' experience with time transcendence, however, helped him to step past some of his own miscreations, or the *part of him that feared and did not love.* I'd struggled myself to understand the nature of miscreation, so Simeon extends his own description, identifying miscreation as thought, form, or essence one creates out of a fear coming from a void that *never was*, because fear doesn't belong in a greater reality. He contrasts our miscreating to God's creating, God having created from a *"precious void,"* as Simeon calls it, from a substance that only contained love, and therefore producing *the creatable.*

THE REMNANT

AUGUST 11

It makes no difference how you receive, but why you receive is of utmost importance. It is a tale of two cities, in one respect you see, that the one would attempt to lord [one city] *over the other, like twins, good and evil, and so the story goes. It is the saga of mankind, the two opposites who share so much in common, you see. It is a motherboard of possibility when it is hardwired or soft-wired into reality, it makes no difference of its kind—it simply is. And so your thoughts are my thoughts. It will change over time. Be patient.*

And that, considering what we have covered about time, is the most ironic of all, that you should exercise patience in order to receive what essentially has already been said. You are way ahead of yourself in one way, and behind in another. And so it is. The cock did crow three times [sic] *on Golgotha that night, and he was never more afraid as much as I then, for my lord had left my sight, and he was no where to be found indeed* [Mark 14:72]. *We searched the streets for him in vain. It was a terrible reckoning place, this evening in the essence of our lives, for we each fell prey to the hellish existence, the crux of our* [own] *weaknesses, and the chains of our experience all wound into one. Much happened that night that is not told. And the time to tell it will come in the future, the near future, to be sure. "If only" is only a heartbeat away from you at any moment in your coursing here on earth, as was mine that evening the cock sang its merry song. It was not a good morning. We were sore afraid, you see, each going his own way searching, searching and feeling far from complete. We were not ready for what we beheld, and yet, we were the instigators of what we beheld and became. And so it is and always will be.*

I would like to digress just one more time if you will, and tell you a story of great import for the Master's souls. This is a group, you see, that have in their care a remnant of mankind that still walks the earth today, to the north, not far from Golgotha, this place where the cock crowed. In this remnant there are speakers who would take more of what it means to soar in one's energetic face, to create in one's energetic right. They might be called druids, of a sort—but they are the ones who will never see another stance besides the one they share now in their presence of mankind. You must know them over time, for they are the ones in right of His majesty and glory, and what this means is simply that they know of Him to greater extent than perhaps the newer age groups would care to know. Platitudes will not work with these people; they know their stations in life well, and are determined to walk in freedom of thought regarding their Master and Lord. To that extent, you do well to emulate them in this freedom of thought, but not in everything that they do. More on these druids will come later.

I asked Simeon for clarification about the message from the moon on July 27.

The moon is the source of life in the night in so many ways. The light has saved many, and continues saving many species, creatures, and lower life-forms. Its energy speaks volumes for the essence of lunar creations, and in them shines the essence of pathways into greater civilizations. Lunar is imagination, and its imaginary properties strike each one of you as you sleep and dream. The special message that this lunar light sends out is available for you every night, but scarce many of you take the time, or perhaps, have the knowledge of its capabilities in that realm. The lunar message is this: take stock of the night, and behold that I am in focus as you will me to be. I hang high here above and beyond you to take stock of all that I have to give, and you give back to me with your focus, be it just for a single moment.

Moon gazing is a specialized tradition for all souls, whether we make a habit of it or not. The moon has certainly fascinated mankind for centuries, and holds the attributes of the gods, but its special message remains and maintains in the very structure of your souls, [and] the yin of your flesh is bound up in its lunar essence, more than you know. Moonshine is absolutely crucial for your deeper essence of sleep and dreaming, you see. Its special message is one that you should never forget, as long as you shall live. Yes, it is likened to a marriage of lights. And its light is the feminine side of day.

Did the radiance of Moses really occur? How did he really appear when he returned to his tribe?

Dermatomes are of a purity block—a magnification of cellular structure in pulses over time. So the cell flickers, if you will, in and out of existence. This is nothing new to you. Cell essence can now be better understood in the nature of quantum energy, and casts a future probability of knowing further why dermatomes behave in the manner they do, for one. Of course, many questions will be answered as this knowledge of true cellular structure comes forth. The cell's mitigation between life and death is a narrow one; the eye of the needle, with the camel walking through it, this is the behavior of cellular dermatomes as I would like to explain to you [Matthew 19:24].

Moses had an unleashed mitigation of cellular release in time, transcending time and glorifying all that he had fought to believe in, it passed before his eyes in a flash of recognition. Thus he was changed. The dermatomes with which he sat before Yahweh were changed in this flash, and this was what the people marveled by; this reorganization of dermatologic structure. In a flash, he was reorganized in such a way, his face was, his body was, that no man could recognize him as the man he was before. He had completely changed. It was more than just aging and wizening, in a sense, although that was a major feature. It was a restructuring of major cellular structure, in that his facial characteristics were not altogether the same. He had switched some for others, so to speak, and this was in part what baffled those below who later beheld him. Dermatomes can be represented in the nature that they are always shifting, one for the other, slightly up-long and down-long as they progress through life. In this shifting, you will find that one sequence is as necessary for the other, for the skin to fold is disruption of sequence, and to fold again, further disruption, you see. So aging could otherwise be spoken of as a disruption of the dermatomes, period.

Lessons come about in a marginal existence when the heart is not informed by its center of all that it has for abundance. This is at the hub of fear. Its intention cannot be understated, the heart's intention. It can be overstated. It brings true Source forward to meet friendship at all levels. We will discuss more on this friendship at a later time. For now, be replete in all that you do, and you will be blessed. Sayonara.

When Simeon mentions, *"So the cell flickers, if you will, in and out of existence. This is nothing new to you,"* I think he is referencing a startling experience I'd had about six months before the date of that session. We were on a family vacation, and our teenage niece was with us. We'd had an exciting day and I was tossing and turning, trying to get to sleep. Finally I was about to nod off, but for some reason, I opened my eyes and glanced around our hotel room. At that instant, the sleeping lump on the cot who was my son (then six), simply vanished from sight. Before I could recover from that, our niece (then sixteen) vanished as well. Next came my husband, all of this in a matter of a split second—then me. I blinked, and everyone was back again. Had I merely dropped off to sleep? I don't know. The order of disappearances occurred from youngest to eldest. It's been long noted in certain esoteric circles that an older (adult) earthbound being's spirit is more invested in bodily form than a younger (child). We each vanished in the order of our investment, it seemed.

Simeon's allusion to *the cock did crow three times* during Simon Peter's denial of Christ does not coincide with the writings of Mark [Mark 14:72], which states that Peter denied knowing Christ three times before the cock crowed twice.

From a rooster standpoint, it's very plausible that there were even many roosters crowing during the crucifixion. The nature of the longer, five-minutes-plus rooster crow is circadian, typically occurring at nightfall, and again from about 3 a.m. to sunrise. However, a rooster may crow repeatedly if challenged by another male—in shorter intervals. Simeon adds other identifiers like, *on Golgotha that night,* and *that evening the cock sang its merry song. It was not a good morning.* There are discrepancies between the Gospels about exactly when Peter recognized he was fulfilling Jesus' prophecy by denying him.

According to Dionysius the Areopagite, angels were the first to receive Divine radiance, also known in the Jewish tradition as the *shekhinah,* or the feminine face of God. Scholars still argue whether Moses manifested this radiance, or *shekhinah*, himself.

In explaining Moses' facial changes as *an unleashed mitigation of cellular release in time*, Simeon is addressing this historical event as one of a quantum nature, which theorizes that all objects we identify around us as separate are truly connected, sharing vortices of energy in an interconnected and interpenetrated web of life. Did Moses have an understanding of and ability to manipulate these energetic fields? I think it's highly likely he did.

More anachronistic sayings! While the concept of a motherboard points us toward computer technology and electronic processing, it was an interesting discovery to find out that "hardwired versus soft-wired" can also refer to biological processing, or the concept that our minds can continuously switch between unconscious and conscious states of thought and perception. We will hardwire certain activities in our thoughts if we feel they will continuously recur.

CLARIFICATION

AUGUST 14

I've decided to loop back through some of the older material for clarification. I don't want to interrupt the unfolding process of other material, so I will alternate between clarifications of the very early material and receiving new material. I've had to look for an opportunity to sit for a session this week. Tonight I'm getting out here later, about 9:45 p.m. As I prepare the computer and light a candle, I clearly hear, "Ten percent."

April 30:   *This field is a network of lines central that go behind open judgment.*

May 7:   *They went further like it from time to time; they went back and forth somewhat like the one before.*

May 9:   *We are noticed in comfort; a fish swims, birds feed themselves, the cycle continues. Start looking out for this. Connect and hold. The air speed—that none of that is written, is mapped: this little boy will save many. Watch how he writes. In front of him especially is a train of thought he must follow. Be the yielder. Give him room. There is space for you both. Yield.*

What follows are Simeon's comments on these first obscure sessions:

These originals were of a proper order of such, the trines not given as yet, for you had to come to a place where the taking thereof was more automatic import. It seems that when you first start or commence, the sentence will spiral out of control, I know, and you are shaping it after a fashion in perhaps your own heart, or immediate thought process, it is for this you worry.

And so, tonight, I will start by answering your questions. Lines behind open judgment are just that, you see. They are lines or fields of thought that have been left open to the judgment of their ways. While this may not make perfect sense or unfold into your language just as a dock may not greet the water on all occasions, and should not, herein is the answer to your question in toto [in total]. *The lines themselves are right for a season, while you have them import in sequence, one from the other, and then they go behind judgment, you see, or are subject to the most exquisite form of interpretation, depending upon the language which they must be adapted to. This was the forerunner to your melding these thought processes together in sentence form, to hear the words stutter one after the other, one by one, in a most absurd fashion at first. These lines behind open judgment, you see, were the ones left to you to come forward, the ones in your thoughts, which are my thoughts, and so that* [they] *could connect together in intelligible fashion. Otherwise, this book would ne'er have begun. It was simple to import to you the meaning of this statement, as you are currently taking this dictation now. Lines behind open judgment also reserves for itself or themselves a yet deeper meaning. These are field lines in your universe, unlike other universes, in the fashion in which they are communicated and spared, often before they are even said, uttered, or spoken [in] any fashion. These are the judgments which you are forced and compelled to make in order to survive this planet, you see. This field is open in that you are constantly reckoning on the right response, the appropriate answer. This will become clearer as you progress along these lines, these tones of frequency with which you are able to receive my full sentences at the moment.*

As for the boy, he is your son, indeed. He will not write with the eloquence you have; he does not care that much for it. It will not be enforced upon him as it was upon you. He will not therefore suffer in the same way you have for it. However, he has in his own right of way how he wishes to communicate in finer tones, and so he will. You must listen carefully to what he speaks, for it has to say far more than you often give it credit. Be willing to hear him, and you shall receive what is needed for your souls. He isn't perfect—he isn't a messiah, either— but he is one who has a code of salvation upon his lips that he will discover in the pathway of how you are raising him now. He shall utter his first broad statement in a few days, then weeks, then months. It is for this that you must prosper in all that you do. This, again, may sound strange on the surface, but it will become clearer as we go along. Prospering, you will remember, has nothing to do with what one garners in terms of earthly success or material find. He will succeed in far greater things, the one who hearkens to the voice from which all things sprang forth. His ear is already tuned well. Allow it to remain so tuned with as little confusion as possible.

Quite soon you will satisfy yourself that you have indeed heard well, that this hearing of yours is not impaired in either world, in God's eyes. In your own, you may falter from time to time, wandering and waxing thin in your attempts to decipher the intricate meanings of my words, when they don't seem to fit the agenda you have carved for yourself. Remain open, and this, too, will come to you. It is of utmost importance that you tune carefully from here on out. To tune, sit quietly for at least one minute, allowing the words to fly past, until you fix upon a single word that makes a good starting place. You have done this well so far, but at times you are concerned about this takeoff point. If you will set for yourself a habit of how you will tune, you will trust it more. One minute, or one second, is totally unnecessary. Remember, this awareness and translation occurs outside of time. You have no more need to wait one minute to one hour. It shall pass to you regardless.

Hearken not to the things of fleshly concerns when you are making your attempts to maileron into a devoted sequence of time for your soul. What this means simply is [to] know your master [God] well, and attune to the One well, the One who is at your service. You cannot serve two. You are commenced here to serve the One. His will is yours, regardless. So the will that serves flesh is and never was yours. It is a façade. Facades walk and eat and drink and make merry on a daily basis, all the while unrealized in their deeper necessities of living, so to speak, about the next breath, the way the breath turns to make its journey deep within, that these precious gifts are yours in spite of the facade. They are one in the same with life breath and yet not connected, so through the material or physical gain of the body, it is turned from its inception, coursing through your veins as life force, and yet no longer necessary in your physical terms for any life outside of its own. Let me see here, this is a difficult one: this life breath that courses through your veins, each and every one of you, this individual source of life segmented through the millions populace of all mankind, and creatures, and sentient beings of every shape and form—this life breath is the antithesis if the matter which formed at its inception forgets the matter, leaves the body behind—yet this life breath will go on into infinity and from infinity. This, you see, is the hope that all mankind is to rest upon: this life force that stoops to serve the individual need, yet compresses itself further down to meet the very seedbed of all nature, and hence rises above all that matter would attempt to contain. It cannot be contained in any way, shape, or form, not [within] *the yin* [in] *your body, nor mine, nor any of that which creeps and crawls the earth. In this soul, spirit—though fleshly gratitude we may find—life breath does not touch that which is fleshly, in the end, but hovers alongside it for the rest of its natural earth life in earth years. Half this life is not enough to capture what it means to live one's days in duty to the flesh, yet more than most spend half this life doing just that. Herein we are slaves to our flesh until it teaches us that there is, and always was, more. Amen.*

A trine is a term used in astrology and represents an aspect formed when a planet, point, or other celestial body is 120 degrees away from another planet, point or celestial body. Considered to be highly beneficial aspects, trines instill fortune on those individuals who have them in their natal or progressed horoscopes. The idea is the personality experiences a free flow of energy between two planets. If there is a negative characteristic of a trine, it is that a trine can possibly present a personality with such giftedness, he or she may be predisposed to be unchallenged and therefore, lazy.

When Simeon discusses *"this life breath that courses through your veins*, and yet, *cannot be contained in any way,"* he is talking about the mystery and near formlessness of life breath, something that can be used as a point of focus during meditation for quieting the mind. Becoming deeply aware of breathing—being able to identify the breath's turn, or the brief point in which breathing ceases to travel one way in order to flow in another—can generate a particularly heightened state of consciousness.

The same is true of an athlete endeavoring to gain muscular strength by weight training. During each lift, the muscle experiences two turns from a concentric (lifting or moving the weight against gravity) to eccentric (resisting the weight against gravity) contraction. An athlete who strives to fine-tune control during these turns, or shifts from lifting to resisting, can acquire a tremendous amount of strength. Paying particular attention to these shifts from expansion to contraction is key to mastery in both of these illustrations.

Simeon, when he says *"Quite soon you will satisfy yourself that you have indeed heard well,"* speaks aptly about a hearing impairment

I've had since a child and how this has shaped my attitude toward trusting "the form" of things. I grew up second-guessing myself in the world of auditory ability. From an early age, I was keenly aware of the frailty of the human physical form.

MYSTERY OF CREATION

AUGUST 16

I conducted the earlier sessions consistently at night with little variance in the time frame. However, as I continued along, I began occasionally sitting for sessions in the morning. The change in time seemed to make little difference as far as receptivity. I'm receiving the following session in the morning.

Perhaps it will surprise you to know that in the beginning, the substance or all that stood for creation was wrapped in the sinews, so to speak, of One who would not be taken outright for its Creator, in the sense that your Western theology participates. The stories have grown and twisted, to be romanticized by the crust of living, told so many times, that, the sustenance of the stories themselves has gone out and about you—away, very far away.

Do not be disturbed when I tell you, or say that, the Creator did not intend for the created to even know what therefore sparked the tree of life, the inception, the giving of All That Is. This is a mystery, and remains so. It was intended to remain so. The force behind it was intended to be this God, you see, this All Supreme Force, to be sure, that you have attributed Him with powers He does not wish to be attributed. (Let me see, He does not wish to be attributed with the focus with which you give these powers.) For when you focus solely on a single attribute, all of nature falls out of balance already. In this God that you adore and love, and apply all the attributes of creation, you see, you have already lost the major contribution which He himself wished to make; and that was the triloquy of existence, the three in one: and it is the mind, matter, and spirit. This is not the devil's trilogy, as some might insist. It is only when the one of the other becomes, or comes forward, and exists solely of itself, that the devil comes out to play. You are not only mind, only body, or only spirit. You will see manifestations always of the imbalances that occur. For the one in his body, he is an atheist, or a person who knows only pain, and sees the toil of life. For one only in mind, he struggles to accept what is, and looks beyond all things for what might be, and he frustrates himself in that he can never fully know while all is still in the motion of creation and changing constantly. And the one who remarks on the spirit, who spends his life devoted to spiritual things at the expense of applying them to matter, you see, he is no better than the fool who is trapped in this body. And so, the balance of the triloquy. See the difference between these words triloquy and trilogy, and this will be made clear to you.

If I find that a man should not grasp or reap what he has sown in this life, he can surely know that the end will come for him in the same fashion as it would had he felt for all his days the smile of his Creator, and known Him intimately. For the existence of the triloquy shows no favor man to man. Each must follow his lines of existence, balancing the three as best he can for that lifetime, to be sure fraught with error from time to time, but ever emerging into one with the other, forming always into the mass energy force that left mankind to his own devices, according to some. That is not the entire truth. It very much seems so, but it is never so far or close as you will imagine. The triloquy, if you should struggle to attain its meaning, has its origin in sound and song. It is sure to come over to you in time, and travels on waves and frequencies that we all share in common. Thus, mankind can (for short stints) find common ground with others, in this triloquy of existence, before it is thrown off balance again, you see. This emerging of souls one to another is in constant flux, and a creative flux and force behind all that is, and you are emerging of your own devices, yet emerging from all that has constrained and restrained the energetic force behind matter from the beginning of time. Supreme dogma or power? Not so. The constraints and restraints are simply the influx and reflux of matter itself, or energy itself, in reaction to another state of balance or imbalance, you see. In this sound you may find that, in its inception, as with all inception, it tries to have as its focal [beginning] a fulcrum existence; that is, it moves along lines which are tethered to other planes to shift and pole-vault the stately tune of choice into existence. It is this way with sound. For you to know and understand this is of utmost importance to attaining what you so greatly desire. Hearing cometh by the Maker of this fulcrum existence, and you, in essence, are the fulcrum. Have you forgotten the function of a fulcrum? Go look it up. The axis is integral only in that it must apply force in the right direction, not the other way around. See what you can see in this, and you will be blessed.

When Simeon introduces *the balance of the triloquy* as not being *the devil's trilogy*, I believe he is alluding to the way the essence of mind, matter, and spirit operate in this dimension by his specific usage of the word triloquy. A triloquy is a dramatic convention generated from the word soliloquy. A soliloquy is a dramatic stage monologue that is addressed to oneself. Any asides to the audience are not necessarily heard or even noticed by other characters onstage. A triloquy, therefore, is a soliloquy for three. This asserts the possibility that any of the three can become caught up in its own dramatic monologue to the exclusion of the other two. This exclusion prompts imbalance in one's nature, so that the entire human entity is not acting together as a unit—mind, matter, and spirit.

In a 2004 study, neuroscientists identified that phoneme perception plays a crucial role in language processing. A phoneme is a minimal, contrasting unit that may be pronounced in more than one way in the sound system of language. Scientists investigated the possibility that infants had inborn access to phonemic representations before the ability to learn syllables and other patterns of speech. This study in particular identified that triloquy effects are also properties associated with phoneme perception.

In a 1990 study by Pitt and Samuel, scientists found that English-speaking subjects could narrow their attention to precise phonemic positions inside spoken words. The authors proposed that phonemes, rather than syllables, are the primary units of speech perception and initiate the ability to discriminate words. This study was repeated with the same results in 1997 (Christopher Pallier) using French-speaking subjects.

A trilogy, by contrast, is defined as a set of three works of art in literature, drama, or film that are connected in theme or authorship, and may be viewed as a single work, or three individual ones. Perhaps Simeon is saying that the existence of mind, matter, and spirit can and has been dissected in this way, and viewing them as a triloquy is truer to how the mind-body-spirit collaborates into one unit.

In understanding what Simeon means by *fulcrum existence*, we must consider the three classes of levers: first, second, and third. The fulcrum forms the axis along a lever, or becomes the point located between the input effort and the output load. When force is applied either by pushing or pulling the lever, the fulcrum acts as the center point. An example of a first-class lever is a seesaw. In second- and third-class levers, the fulcrum is relocated to the end of the lever, opposite the input. In the third-class lever, the fulcrum is attached to the lever, and the input load is greater than the output load. Examples of second- and third-class levers are a diving board and a pair of tongs, respectively.

I recognized maileron as a manufactured word, wondering if perhaps Simeon had meant "aileron" instead. I asked him to elaborate.

Maileron is a manufacture only in its essence of sending forth an important message to you on airstreams that often require a roll in balance. You incorporate an aileron tendency as you mete out and sort through the impulses which I give you for words to develop. You've got mail, so to speak. The rolling which you must handle in forethought as you type it as dictation on the page is difficult for you; you as yet would rather hear them [words] one for one rather than find them rolling into your brain. Thus, my comment about maileron tendencies in your work of late. This, however, is productive in taking you where you need to be to find more confidence in what I have to offer you each time you commit to this hour with me. It makes no difference, night or day, morning or twilight; I am here and always here for you. It is the nature of my essence in this place with no time, you see. And so it is with many of us, tending to different tasks in a fashion which you cannot understand in your world of constraints. Restrain no more, we would say. In the world where you are bound by so many things (especially these things such as time and space), true freedom can be found in the essence of sparing a moment for yourself each day to shift your focus from that which breathes in time as essence to that which breathes out time as no essence. This is a difficult task for you to do while you live from day to day, its mastery a marvel still among cultures that devote whole lives to its study and mastery. You have only just begun, and begun to see what such a state can do for you. It mitigates the three (triloquy) in such a way that no other plan of atonement can do. So therefore, follow the lines of reasoning that impart to you what you must know about becoming still and silent in your soul each day, however brief that moment may seem. Find one and take it. Truly let the moment go, and its essence will fill your life with peace. Amen.

Finding the moment in which you can do this is like finding a needle in a haystack, or so it seems. Worries encroach even into sleep at times. So to master the one-second moment can be a lifetime endeavor indeed. The reason for doing so is a mystery in its own right, but can be explained as thus: The moment you lie in wait for your soul "on the other side" is lost to the moment you have here to find your soul on this side. This finding oneself at last occurs at in any place and time and in all place[s] *and time*[s]*. And when you have found yourself, you are already on your way to becoming someone else. Such is life and breath. So cherish the moment outside of time that you may find each day you live, and remember that no matter how brief it may seem, it is yours forever.*

I think it's interesting to compare Simeon's description of *maileron* with the typical word usage of the word *aileron. Aileron* is a French word meaning "little wing." Most fixed-winged aircraft have ailerons, which are hinged surfaces that are attached to the trailing edges of the wings. The ailerons control an aircraft during roll, with one going down while the other goes up, for example one dropping the left wing while the other raises the right for a turn, or pitch, left.

Chapter Four

The Others

As I come to this morning's session, I am troubled by the true meaning of illusion, perception, and reality as given in *A Course in Miracles*. Perhaps Simeon will comment on that, but that again will force us away from reviewing the things he has said before. But, as I have noticed with any number of the sessions, my emotional needs behind the thoughts of the moment can attract what needs to be received, or what Simeon sometimes chooses to address.

In the system of [the] others, you will find that the meaning of light and dark may and can give or bring sudden shifts of thought and meaning [both] akin and far removed from your own. This system of others of which I speak is a metrigal [sic] system at best, it is a reality not far removed from your own which exists just outside your own in deep space, as it were, but it is fond of making its encroachments upon your own. This system of stars and galaxies and universes outside your own is the mass of which you have known before, in your earlier time, as it were, in your system. It propagated the existence of dinosaurs and other earlier life-forms that existed on this planet. But all mass must change and migrate over time and existence, continual creative existence, you see. This system outside your own, this other reality, so to speak, is one in which you will not find a force of kindness and benevolence for its own sake; it will stake out what is good and true in your system, and feed upon it. I am not talking about sin or evil of such. And I am not talking about life's good turns, or attributes of wisdom, or kindness—I speak of that which propagates life here, the life force is that which the other system seeks out. We are the center of God, on the one hand, and yet His energy transmigrates out to these other systems in the other, you see. His reality here is not His reality there. You would struggle to understand such a reality with Him in that other system. That was your dream of late. (I'd had a dream where I found myself at cross-purposes with the religious overtones in the sequence of events; I'd also had difficulty seeing in this dream.) *It is difficult to see and understand the forces at work, both here and there. Some seem so terribly evil, while others so delightfully benign. Some are cloaked and daggered, so to speak. But in this all, you see, I want you to understand the forces, plural, at work. It is not merely two: good and evil. These are categories you have given to simplify what you behold on this plane. There are outside forces that stand around this universe—still the forces, or works of the creator God, the All That Is —but these forces come in conflict at times with what goes on in your immediate vicinity. It creates wars and rumors of war. It creates violence of every kind known to man. Yet it creates the untroubled birth of a baby bird and gives it wings to fly. So, you see, it is this transmigrating of energetic forces that you cannot simply understand as polar extremes; they wash against each other like water in your plane, both cleansing and soiling all in their path. One brings life, another brings life impeded, and another may bring death—all in various degrees. Purity is hard to find, for the creative processes require that all of the energies combine. And so, the ever-present struggle to find checks and balances of all that forces itself upon your matter from without and within.*

Straddle the two [realities of good and evil], *and you would see the perfect love from whence all came. Straddle the two categories of realities which you have created for yourself in order to explain all that is, without fully explaining it, indeed. Thus, when you study of illusion, reality, and perception, yours is a difficult study indeed. For in one is the other, and all are combined. Until you stand outside of one reality, you cannot see the other in its fullest intensity. And yet, they blend in ways which you would not expect them to. Thus, in idealistic terms, you would stretch for one over the other; reach for one over the other. Yet this is not so. They are twins—one evil, one good, but both from the same inception, in your category. In God's category, they were both necessary to find life, and the existence that sprang forth thereof, the generations of species of animal, plant, and human—were all a part of this necessary blend. The extremes which you point to—the evil and the good—these extremes are magnifications of creations already set firmly in place, yet transmigrated from other mixtures of reality and energy. You cannot hold onto the extremes when you finally realize that everything is truly in constant change. And so, your perceptions as they are now will not be so tomorrow, and tomorrow. Even the most rigid of mental structure and thought is impressed upon by these realities from without and within in such a way that over time, these souls will not deny that something, indeed, has happened* [changed] *around them. So it is.*

Unbending thoughts given by substructures like me, for that is what we are in this existence now—unbending thoughts are cacophony of creativity that ride on field waves for your acceptance. These waves are often hard to capture, you see. They mix and roll and confuse many. That is why I speak of unbending versus circular reasoning—it is this you grapple with when you take this text. Mine is unbending—it shoots straight from the hip and yet rolls in over a tide of frequency that may find you transposing a word here and there for your own convenience of understanding. This is all right, although distortions may occur in [your] *time, and many. These categories can be corrected at any time you wish, until the rolling tide is mastered—for channeling, too, requires mastery. You are doing well, believe it or not!*

Unbending lines of thought are unyielding from the substructure from which they are sent. They yield not for the refrains of tide and flux in frequency, as do your own conversation. I know this seems opposite [of the way things are], *but after all, you are learning that in your own world, your perception really is upside down!*

Besides a vivid discourse concerning our human need to categorize our world in good and evil terminology, Simeon here explains how the admixture of the two energies we commonly and critically separate in our minds is necessary for ongoing life. Likewise, the difficulty in communicating with other realms happens, in part, because of this admixture of creativity.

THE LORD'S PRAYER

As an ordained interfaith minister, I'm occasionally asked to bless a meal or offer an invocation. I asked Simeon for some short prayers for such occasions:

In the words of Simeon Peter:

> *Take heart in all that you do; it is for the benefit of all mankind and God's will that you speak forth from All That Is, the life and breath force; All That Is, God, the One with No Name, is sent round about you in every moment you live and breathe, for all eternity. A man or woman is no obstacle to him or herself when he or she breathes the essence of All That Is, and this occurs simultaneously with every breath ever taken. This union is undeniable, and cannot be earned or recouped in any fashion. It simply is, and always was. You must recall it for yourself when you forget. Simply by this:*

Our Father, Who art in Heaven,
Hallowed be Thy name. Thy kingdom
come, Thy will be done, on earth as it is
in Heaven. Your breath and bread are
ours today. Let us remember always that
the temptation of ourselves, clothed in an
unrighteousness that we perceive, is not
Your will, and never was. For we with
You are the glory forever. Amen.
[Variant: Matt. 6:9–13, Luke 11:2–4]

In the words of Simeon Peter:

Betwixt and between is the place for
each and every one of you as you
traverse the earth in our glory of God.
For you see, His light is ours, His life is
yours, and you are the extension and the
extenders of all He has to give. Be not
afraid in all that you do, and you will be
blessed indeed. Amen.

In the multiple faces of life energies and forces, you will find it
true that, this good and evil will begin to fade and blend into what God
sees as the necessary turns of the tide for balance in all of nature and

life. Even the most trifling of human slights and resulting indignation as such is a necessary part of what keeps the earth spinning in the right direction. The forces of thought and the many trains of thought [and their impact] on matter, you do not perceive how you truly effect them at their core. One day you will. It does not have to happen outside of time as you know it. It is difficult, but it can be done. Others have done it before you. Rest now.

My shoulder and left wrist continued to bother me from time to time. The wrist was beginning to throb at that point, and I ended the session. Later in the day I found myself thinking that I'd like to come back and clarify metrigal, for one, and some of the other-worldly content, good and evil, as well as the prayer content, particularly the use of the traditional Lord's Prayer with its variants.

AUGUST 20

I'm receiving this session inside the house, not the cabin. We'll see if anything comes forward. I'm remembering Simeon's instructions: A childlike place of joy, one minute of free-flowing thoughts, then a word of inception.

Formularies: they may seem right for the standard of the time, but are not more than the stake of their concerns. You see, the code which rests upon the formulae themselves is bound upon a constant flow of words and symbols rich in language that flow from top to bottom of a single signal, or siglet, in the moment it is released from your minds. This is the course of language, and all languages, that you shall meet in this earth. I say these things because, you see, the freedom to choose another outlet at any time is bound in your minds and words, and thoughts: it is circular reasoning, with its inception on your lips at the same time it ends. This is the course of thought from the beginning of the first one to the end of the last one. [This could imply several meanings: the first and last thoughts on earth, as well as the first and last thought in any given sentence or conversation.] *And as you have read, there is truly no beginning or end for all of mankind. Surely there is, and was, a beginning of man as he coursed in human form, and an end thereof, as well—but this is only one of the many forms you will take in this formula we call time.*

Therefore you shall speak these things as you will, and they shall never encroach the way you [ultimately] *live, you see, for it is a table-turner to speak of that which you know not, is this not so? And yet, this is your state of Being for all time, this speaking of that which you do not fully know. Thus you speak of that which you believe you have known, believe you have been told, believe you have learned, ascertained; do you see how much of your entire existence walks on faith and trust? And yet, you desire to know God. The antithesis, it is the antithesis of coursing these thoughts through your brain, this faith, you say, to accept by faith that which you do not know, to trust that which you have not seen, and yet, you do it every day. You base the road that you will follow to town, for instance, upon your past experience that it will exist tomorrow, but do you know, absolutely know, that it will still exist tomorrow? And when you strike out on such a journey, do you stop to question its existence? No, for the most part, you do not. And so it is the way of life, this existence which you take upon faith, and not the knowing thereof. Thus you will know God in no other way, first and foremost, than from those beliefs you have swirled through your thought processes, much like the road you follow into town. Does this disturb you? It should not cause you to lose your way. Instead, it is written for your more complete understanding of what is meant by, "Take faith, take heart, and with courage move through life as you know it to be." Amen.*

Metrigal is the point in which all things consume each other; it is the meeting point of all energetic varieties and tonal frequencies. Therefore, yes, the metrical [metrigal] tendency in accumulation over time, as it appears in your world.

Take heart. Metricality accumulates, and therefore, your ability to understand the words of late; this too, will improve, for time is truly on your side in all regards.

I've always wondered about variants to the Lord's Prayer. In the traditional Western translation, God is addressed as being "out there" while we remain earthbound moderators. Simeon's variation indicates something new afoot, that we are somehow less separated from the Heavens or our Heavenly Father than we originally thought. In Neil Douglas-Klotz's *Prayers of the Cosmos: Meditations on the Aramaic Words of Jesus*, an early Aramaic text begins the Lord's Prayer:

"Radiant One: You shine within us, outside us—even darkness shines—when we remember . . ."

Historically, formularies were medieval collections of models for the execution of public or private documents, or what we today call forms or templates. Simeon seems to be saying that, while forms are functional and can, of course, be contractually binding, they are only specific to their narrow focus of concerns. While forms are designed to help us understand the nature of our responsibilities or obligations, they are rigid structures that cannot apply in every situation for all time.

A siglet, on the other hand, is a modern-day communicator of change. In computers, it is a dashboard widget that communicates with an ampsig, feeding it the information to display onscreen. It sends information about updates as well as how long the computer has been running.

Chapter Five

Flavius Josephus

It's been a three-week hiatus, so I'm unsure how Simeon will proceed. The break partially occurred because of discouragement from, I assume, some well-meaning people. I consider it an early-warning system that his words could provoke some while inspiring others.

In some manner you shall be the giver and the receiver of this text over time, this material you gain by insight from another, namely me, and you shall not fret when the time comes to hand it over still. Of great import to you and to those around you is the nature of this text, which you shall come to trust over time. It is in this nature that you shall give of yourself to it, that you shall not find in it what you had originally felt would be there waiting for you. Such is life, and all that lives, in the search for its kind. There was a man who, on the outset of his journeys, would pick a special place to say his prayers each morning before the sun would rise; he was a foreign man, by your terms, and what he would have to say about his lord, even more foreign still. This was a man of great import in his country at the time, and some called him Josephus; the text you have concerning him already will do. However, this place for his prayers was later found inadequate by those who came to follow him because these places had not the import they originally had for him, you see. Josephus was a man of great character for his day, and in the hour that he whispered his prayers to his God, he meant each and every word, with great care. The language is not far from yours in its supplicatory fashion—he prayed for most anything he wished, and not according to any dialogue of the day. This, therefore, made his special place, this Josephus, and his prayers, for they came not out of obligation, nor concerns greater than he should care for himself; he prayed truthfully and steadfastly, and that was all that was required of his special place. It barely had the shade of a tree, and was far from the most comfortable location he could have made, but it afforded him a view that kept him mindful of why he came, and why he later left, and what he had to do. Josephus is the heralder of prayers, and those who would follow him will learn how to find their own special places. These coordinate points come from such places. You adorn them with your thoughts, your words, and your intentions time and time again. So holy places become not because they are declared that way by God, but from the energy transmissions of the souls that pass through the coordinate points, who ride on the coordinates, if you will, to carry out the will of their Father, their Om, you see. Josephus was a great man in respect of his helpful wanderings and wonderings before God. Amen.

Supplement this activity always with what you give yourself by daylight. You must forward yourself into the evening with the hope and promise of receiving that which you may find, on the outset, as obscure as the material of your dreams. Clarity comes with practice and daily preparation. Do what your soul finds delight in doing, and you will have a good start. As for your shoulder, it is despicable that you should carry on with it any longer. A cure comes soon. You will see. Wait for a fortnight, and it will be clear to you what you should do.

The fortnight turned out to be a little over a month. Simeon gave me specific instructions in October about how to cure the shoulder inflammation I'd been experiencing. Within fourteen days [fortnight] from that session however, a massage therapist did suggest that the inflammation appeared to be originating in my neck.

The name Josephus I recognized as corresponding to Biblical times. After briefly researching Josephus, I found that he did write a book of prayers. I later acquired *The Works of Flavius Josephus*, which include his autobiography, *Antiquities of the Jews, The Wars of the Jews, Flavius Josephus Against Apion,* and *Discourse to the Greeks Concerning Hades.* It strikes me that this material given by Simeon Peter above would've been controversial at the very least in that Josephus was branded a traitor and liar by some historical references. At an early age he immersed himself in Essene teachings, later becoming a Pharisee. When Josephus speaks of building a place of prayer in *Antiquities of the Jews,* 14:257–58, scholars seem to agree that, while rabbinic in nature, Josephus's ideas were also influenced by Greek culture. Today, a place of prayer could more likely occur in "the building of the heart," or is determinable by the state of one's psyche. Several scholarly texts provide analyses of Josephus's views on prayer and his use of prayer within the narrative context of his works. In particular, Josephus's conception of prayer seems at times to be centered on man rather than on God [AP II, 197], that we should ask God not to give us blessings but to give us the capacity to receive them. This view parallels a motif found in Cynic diatribes [*Horace*, Odes 1:31]. In order to receive more light (or answers to certain types of prayer) we need room for more light.

SEPTEMBER 10

So I will ask Simeon tonight for clarification of his last passage and see if there is anything more forthcoming on Josephus and his exemplary prayers.

From the Source, in essence, you are obtaining the metricality you will need to further your understanding of such things as the prayers of Josephus, and all that he has come to mean in history as you know it. Josephus was a man of rare virtue (in the texts this has been obscured to a degree) and will continue to exist as such in your history. He was a madrigal of sorts and he made every attempt to understand and uncover this Jesus that we knew, the one we called upon as our Savior, but not in the way that it has been construed in the present in so many ways. This Jesus, you see, was a madrigal himself. And I can tell by your hesitance to take it forthwith that you should perhaps, too, look this word up. It is familiar to your ears, but its meaning at the moment you have not. Look for meaning especially in the second usage, and all will be made clear concerning this Josephus, and Jesus as well.

Do not clutter your mind with doubt any longer. It is unnecessary on so many fronts that I do not care to explain. You must rest when you can, and allow the thoughts to free-flow. In this exercise, you will find more of me than you thought you could know. It is [necessary], *this letting go of all that stands in your way, these doubts of any sort, that encroach upon your mind or health or wealth, or that form any impediments which you persist in maintaining in this life. It sounds preposterous to the untrained ear, but you have been trained by now. You can trust me when I say that all these barriers can be torn away in a heartbeat, in a moment's breath. That is all for now. Go find your way to madrigal.*

Madrigal is defined as a secular vocal musical composition, popular during the Renaissance and early Baroque eras. Being polyphonic and instrumentally unaccompanied, madrigals featured several voices, usually three to six, and sometimes as many as eight. Madrigals were best known to feature poetry musically, and began around the 1520s in Italy, following in England and Germany in the late sixteenth and early seventeenth centuries. These compositions were through-composed, with the music being annotated to best express the sentiment of each line of poetic text.

While I can't say that Simeon's dialogue in the previous two sessions has been completely clarified by understanding these words, I believe that if taken symbolically, madrigal would mean that both Josephus and Jesus found themselves in a *group* of voices, or a madrigal performance, in that they participated as one with two or more voices in their life teachings. Different dictionaries provide different second usages. In Webster's, for instance, the second usage implies an Italian love song. It is also secular music by nature.

SEPTEMBER 13

This morning I had a client cancellation, so I will try a session at 10:35 a.m., because the nights have been busy lately. This month has seemed to explode with nighttime meetings, gatherings, and goings on of every sort.

The choice to move forward with this text will always and only be yours, in a sense, and yet be mine, as well. This is the essence of a madrigal, the multiple voices sung without accompaniment, or any other source of rhythm or instruction. Certainly a conductor may be applied, but in their nature, and in history, the voices worked in unison off the breath. Unless one has sung in such a feature, he or she cannot understand how it is to operate in such a function of voices.

So, you see, I used this illustration of Josephus and Jesus to encourage you that you have found a way to compile my words into your own structure of existence, and that you have no need to fear whether it is this voice or that voice, mine or yours. It is a madrigal of sorts, even the words you choose to repeat that you feel are of your own, they are of this madrigal, this cacophony of breath and life and sound. So do not fear any longer. I cannot emphasize this enough. You have been brave, to be sure, to assert yourself this far. Now we must go on to other things. We must leave you and your fears in order to make use of the time we have together wisely. And thus it is so.

In order for one to speak, the vocal chords must vibrate, as you are well aware. But these vibrations come from a source yet unknown to your scientists in such a way that even in the uttered rounds of existence, they are not yet discovered as they will be. These vibrations have a cacophony of existence, and therefore my use of madrigal—they feed off each other—they resound off other voices. So therefore, when someone takes the words right out of your mouth, in essence they do. This stems from the great interweaving of all structure, you see, in that your vocal vibrations carry with them the essence of all that has been, or will, or ever will be. Therefore, my friend, you have no wasted thoughts or words. Nothing is throwaway, in that sense. It all carries with it the essence of the Maker, the Om, the Origin, though in the sense that I give it to you today, there is no time in its inception. It breathes out of a past and a future. It forms and punctuates without time as its barrier.

This is difficult to understand in a world where everything seems so punctuated by time. But the fronds of speech come from the roots of existence, and existence comes from everything and nothing all at once. That is the best I can now give to you concerning the nature of voice and speech, and how it transmits over time and yet, without time.

Do not be overly concerned about my mention of your shoulder. You will find a solution, and it will perhaps surprise you that this was something so easily arrived at, after all these years, which, you see, never existed in the essence you have created for yourself. It is wise to

remain open to the possibility that there is always more, and to seek for
it with all your heart, your essence of feeling, and not only your nature
of thinking. Amen.

Madrigals have not only the intrigue of cueing off the rhythm of the breath, or vocal inflections, or syllabants, but also from musical pitch, as well. I think Simeon's material about cacophonies and the madrigal essence of speech hints at how mental telepathy might work. It's possible that all sentient beings very well might be pulling thoughts and words off a central matrix of sound and speech, resonating in another reality as one, but disguised in a highly discordant manner (cacophony) by its transmission over time and space into this dimension. Simeon again mentions the chronic shoulder pain that I'd had for almost two years: the tendons had continued to snap over the left shoulder blade with any overhead movement and remained inflamed.

Simeon ends the last session with a reminder: to seek something with one's heart is to feel it, or to employ emotion, not just logic. You might say that good things come to those who feel well, not to those who merely think well.

Chapter Six

The Lost Session

Sunday morning I'm back for another session—knowing I'll have obligations into the evening. There are a couple of questions stirring in my mind, and I find myself asking them already to see if Simeon will comment upon them during or after the session. I think from here on out I would feel more comfortable with him delivering his own material first, then continuing with Q & A . . . if I hold up. Sessions this far save for my shoulder haven't been unduly taxing, but sometimes I feel a weariness that is difficult to describe—like a strong, but not necessarily urgent sense that I should be wrapping up or going.

An entire session commenced without my knowing that my power cord was damaged, so that the computer ran on battery until this precise point shortly after I started. I close my eyes during all sessions for light trance, and therefore, I did not know that my computer had shut down until my son interrupted me. This is a lost session. It will be interesting to see if Simeon recovers this one, or another session of the same nature. I hardly remember what he discussed, even after the session—but I feel that if it were repeated, I would recognize it.

September 19

The following day, I returned, trying to get a lead sentence, but something altogether different emerged about *coaching*. This was done by automatic writing, which felt very foreign to me. With eyes opened, I struggled.

In the eternal fortitude of these voices you shall hear, it will make hardly any difference over the course of time, you see, if a word should stray a jot or a tittle [Matt. 5:18], as they already have indeed. One word can and will change the meaning of these entered truths, you are correct. Yet it is for this that the cacophony of voices continue to take their course, this pool of tides, as a resource now and forevermore. Be not dismayed in the days to come, for you shall find that as you heed the one, you heed the other. It is of utmost importance that you should not fret in this manner you have. This only serves to create further hindrance for all that is to come. Now, dictation. We shall take a break from yesterday's session and loop back, if you will, when your computer [cord] is repaired.

Coaching: This lesson is one that I prefer to call by that name. Inevitable in all lives, we cannot be without it [coaching]. It is a symbol of a symbol: that we need and desire, to be entrenched in one's own self-strength can only go so far. Coaching, then, is the heat of all metricular substances that bind us. Coaching—and the layers here— are far more than you make of them. Not mere tutelage, but [the] actual binding of heat, the element that helps bring thought processes into matter or substance.

A metricular reaction is what this is indeed. "My thoughts are your thoughts" is, therefore, not mere idle chatter [Isaiah 55:8]. *In the greatest disparity or argumentation, the heat of quarrels, is coaching. To find these coaching elements will bring a substance that contains peace. Thus, coaching in your terms implies encouragement, challenge, and teaching all rolled into one. That is what we are all about, even in the most disparate of circumstances, the two most diametrically opposed, in the most dire of conflict and war; all* [of these] *come back to coaching.*

I sat for a session the following evening to see if the lost session would be repeated to me, or if anything would commence. I could not even remember the leadoff, or the nature of that session in general. I was at a total loss to extract any of the material from my own mind, and I think this was a significant step for me.

In the dinosaur days of computers when I worked as a freelance writer, I have on occasion lost an entire chapter of writing at a time. In those predicaments I was able to reconstruct the chapter mostly from memory. But this clearly was not happening with the Simeon material. His material on coaching seemed to me to imply that the session could be recovered. He indicates that coaching elements are capable of realigning any apparent disparity of thought, for instance, such that the familiar quote in Isaiah 55:8 does not have to stand as an absolute "not." In a greater reality, he indicates there is no disparity of thought.

I Am Here

I received the computer power source on Thursday evening; Friday morning I sat for a session.

Henceforth you will no longer need to instruct me into your presence; I am here. Simply arrange yourself as you will, wherever you may be, and I will arrive shortly. You may send out a call, but that is not altogether necessary. For the tones of all matter and nonmatter will form and segue together amid themselves in a way that you do not here and now understand. For this purpose you shall continue as you have until the time comes that you no longer need what you have so desperately sought for, the validity of this course.

Now, onward. In the time of Christ there was a metricular substance he often used in his goings on, whether healing, speaking, or in all the things he used in order to touch the lives around him. This metricular substance is not far from what you today use as coal. Its properties are one in the same with such a substance, and how it behaves when the air fuses with it. Coal is from the innermost bowels of the earth, you see, a speck of the origins of all, found on virtually every planet, unknown to your scientists. God is not coal [alone]. Do not mistake the substance for the Creator. But in creating it, He placed in the center of the earth the metricular substance where you see, hear, and come into contact with the Divine, and all that is not matter in your dimension. It seems rather simple, I know, but it contains the metricular substances Christ used to heal and upon which he chose to stand, quite literally, in his greatest times of need.

It is for shame, you think, that so many have lost their lives and limbs in search for this coal. But that is not the case. Their fusion with its substance, the metricular substance, at times, becomes more than the body can bear. It is not death or dismemberment, as you see it. It is of the spirit. The death and dismemberment happens on your plane, as with many other diseases and disasters. But the element in this coal is power or fortitude that you cannot imagine. It is not the coal itself. It is its origin. It is in your bodies and those of all nature and in the environment itself, but in coal, it takes on a slightly different form, that when dispersed, becomes a marker of metricularity.

Jesus wrote on a bed of coal, he stood on it, he walked upon it. It is all around you, you see. Yes, this is the physical element coal, but it is so much more than that. This is one of those surprise elements about which Seth [Jane Roberts] was speaking. It would teach science much more about the earth's origins and human origins than they realize. The substance that dissipates into the air when coal is upturned, while harmful to your physical lungs, in diluted quantities, is an inevitable source of life. It comes from light itself. Call it the kryptonite of your planet. If you were able to capture its chain of events as it is dispersed with air, you would understand the life trail of all mankind. The contagions of all would be at your fingertips. But then, these contagions only occur in time. We have not even considered the metricular forces outside of the time sequence. That is another matter altogether, you see.

When speaking about coal, Simeon seems to be talking about a radioactive process, probably on a much smaller and less harmful scale than that used in fuel production. Coal comes from plant remains preserved by water and mud, and its combustive nature makes it the largest worldwide source of electricity. It has been suggested that the radioactive materials released by coal-fired power plants are more hazardous than nuclear power.

THE CONTINUUM

OCTOBER 4

Many things have interrupted sessions. A large part of it was launching the website www.divinecontracts.com last week. The rest was daily life events. One evening after I lost that session, it came funneling through my head as I lay preparing to sleep. I don't know if we'll continue with that tonight, or with something else. I'm feeling a little clairaudiently challenged these days. While seeing the same clients with the same issues, I have not really put my clairaudient abilities to the test lately.

I will start this session with care, to see if Simeon has anything to offer regarding the lost session tonight, or if I get any feeling in general of his energy directing me in this way.

The channel you have provided thus far has been excellent. Do not fear that you should lose this chance or that—for all these chances will come one after the other in a continuum in your time-space quadrant called earth that you so fondly recognize as home, reality, the only reality you now know, for the most part. In other states you will find yet another meaning of reality, and in these you have not foraged much yet, it is part of your journey into deep space, as it were (much like that of your Voyager *series that you are so fond of watching of late). Now we must digress further into the lost session, the instruments from which it came, and the eternity from which it sprang. It is of utmost importance that you allow it to flow freely as it comes, and not to question that which will run across your mind tonight. It may replicate word for word, or it may diverge into another track altogether, but that is for you to find out at this moment. In a fortnight you will once again come before me at this time, and I will come over to yours, and will speak to you altogether more clearly as you have been hoping for and wishing for this long. Here goes:*

You are in a continuum of time and space that you will roam on this earth in the here and now, and you need not worry that this session or any session would ever find itself truly lost. The energy has come, has gone, has transmuted from one space to the next, but that is for you to realize in that what energy does at its very best is to change. And so, as you take this down, you see, there are million fluctuations in your time-space continuum at the moment. It is not unheard of, that one of these molecular changes would burst forth out and away from your space such that, it could ne'er be retrieved, if it were not for the continuum itself. It exists and will never cease to exist. But the continuum is not time, nor what you know of time and space. They are [the continuum, and time-space reality] *two things different altogether.*

They are as different as night and day, although you entertain both in your reality, you see. And so along this continuum is all that ever was and all that will be. Should it collapse, then you would not cease to contain all that was or ever will be. You would simply contain the continuum in a collapsed state of energy, matter, until the cycle for it to expand again. Collapse in a continuum cycle is not its destruction, or annihilation, and can never be—for energy is eternal.

Now, do your best to hang with me for another few moments. It is hot in there where you are, I realize.

You have caught both the essence and the foressence of what I am attempting to say. The foressence is the following of what I must say before I say it. It is the reversal of time, and this is a word I shall use for it. In this continuum, if you will allow time to run backward, you will find yourself not back where you started again, but further still from the space where you began, you see. For all probabilities will continue to cycle and recycle you until you have found your way to play them out. Therefore, this creative genius is part of your human society. Its free will must cycle through all the vast probabilities in time and continue with them, forward, backward, every which way until you have creatively placed each probability you intended to place within the realm of existence as you now know it. The multiple lives, the multiple existences are a part of this scheme, this story. Therefore you must continue to divide and subdivide time and space into quadrants and microparticles for wherein this can occur. This is the stuff of quantum physics, even if on the surface it may sound somewhat contradictory. And so it is. Thank you for the time you've given to this, and to the new site. I will honor your requests to inform you of particular subjects that would be more enlightening for your audience that you will find. Do not be perplexed at the way things may develop for you, since you have chosen this probable reality. It is one of many. Never forget that. You will have that many more.

The time will come when you are no longer guessing in the forefront about why you are taking this down word for word and wondering what will make its way to you next. I speak simply and plainly, while you are capable of handling much more complex and complicated diction. I speak this way because in the forefront you must know that I Am who I am, and not another. Not you. I speak for Simeon Peter, and I speak for you, and I speak for all mankind—and I speak for the God within. But you must understand that as I speak, the varieties of words chosen from the pool within are not totally my own, nor are they yours, nor are they to be attributed to a dualistic, external God, as it were. These words belong to everyone, even those who may not for many realities therefore yet choose to think or speak them. For you see, reality is ever shaping, as are these words. Therefore, to nitpick over which words are mine or yours is a useless exercise, and unnecessary in completing the project we have together now. Rest and be well.

When Simeon talks about subdividing time into quadrants and space into microparticles, I think he's referring to our efforts to understand time and space by reducing them to smaller—even the very smallest—components. For example, he might be referring to an idea like the horary quadrant used in ancient times for determining time with the sun. To subdivide a microparticle, one would begin with something as small as a speck of pollen or very fine dust.

I can honestly say that I never know what to expect from Simeon. Over time I've become accustomed to the rhythm and banter of his speech, but whenever I think I have him figured out, he'll throw in unusual anachronisms like "here goes" or "reporting."

I received some clairaudient phrases the next day about the meaning behind *foressence*, as Simeon has coined the word. I was busy at the moment with shuttling my son to a karate class, and failed to write these down, thinking I would remember them word for word and write them down as soon as I could, and they're gone now. But perhaps I'll receive a note on this in a future session. I certainly intend to find out more about this mystery, as well.

OCTOBER 5

In words you have received from me, the essence of each in a sense is more than the sum of all parts, and you will find that this essence in all words which you receive will hold true for the same. The meaning is, foressence: the sum of all parts, or all meanings of the words themselves. In this quagmire of late, as you have put it, is the essence of all things sorrowful. You see, the many anxieties that you feel and face are simply translated outward to join with those of all the rest, all others. Hence the oneness of your energies are bound and tied together in this way. However, should one of you choose another direction, say, of releasing a certain amount of anxiety, a breath of relief—that, too, will be transmuted along its way. So therefore the foressence of things is the flora, the plume, the fumes on which the essence rides, the directives they take as they go into the universe or into the world and make their way in cycles of energetic impulses on the waves they ride. This you will find to be absolutely true in every facet of its meaning. You might speak of a floral essence, or the smell that rides before the vision or actualization of such an event, but it is one in the same. It brings with it its totality at last, you see. So in these things I speak of, do not be confused that this foressence is something altogether foreign to your plane; it is the very nature of its being. It may operate on a foreign pattern from time to time, making what you perceive as an unnatural, unheard of phenomenon, the paranormal, if you will, but this is also of the essence surrounding your planet and your galaxy. Without oversimplifying, it is all one in the same. So do not feel like you are taking on something far from you, or near you, either.

I speak lately of these things in this infuriating way in order to coax you to stop categorizing so much. It is your nature you have chosen, I know. It is no longer necessary. It is well ingrained, but no longer necessary.

In a folder you will find the essence of foressence. This folder is a mass storage device that you have at your disposal at any time. You think of a folder as something on your computer or a paper device, but I tell you that this folder is as much a part of your subterranean essence as you are. It is a wealth of knowledge and information regarding you, your past, your future-pasts, if you will. It is all you. And for each of you, it is there. You may access it by fearing little, loving much, and waiting until your bodies have allowed its essence to come your way. More on this later.

Subterranean essence, or the nature of coming from underground, seems to allude to Simeon's earlier statements about coal, a metricular substance "*. . . from the innermost bowels of the earth, you see, a speck of the origins of all."*

At the time of this session, our family was in a quagmire, having to make the tough decision whether or not to leave a community that had been our home for almost twelve years. Beyond this interpretation, I think Simeon's *quagmire* can be translated "the day's troubles," or anything in our daily lives that causes doubt to arise in our minds.

FREE THINKERS

OCTOBER 11

It's almost a week later, and it's been a busy one—out of town over the weekend, then back home, a bi-monthly intuitive meeting. It seems like so many things, and good things, have prevented the possibility of a session, including more clients. I look forward to talking with Elizabeth again on Saturday.

In this way you have been, anipol is the usage we will find for all that has been. In a fortnight you will see yet another anipol, I must mention, and in its darkness and lightness together it will show forth all that you need to complete the task of interpretation. Anipols are consequences of thought and reason, which you will find riding upon the waves of tenure—thought tenure, so to speak—and you will hear more about anipols directly. Let us depart to another course.

Forerunners to your time, men of great choice, came one by one into this existence to bring you the freedom of thought you now enjoy. For a time, this was not so. Men and women alike have and will have their thoughts censored by themselves, discouraging free thinking, free thinkers, and all that is to come with them. It is viewed as a dangerous medium of expression. And so, you worry rightfully in that such expression yields repercussions of a sort. Anipols are out there, you see, to partake of when you have or will receive unjust criticism for what it is you have to say. Go study if you must, but they are readily available for your disposal and usage. You can choose how to use them, whether to use them, and when to dispose of them altogether. The properties in which they operate or function in your time are on wavelengths of interpretation or in interpretative devices used by the mind, not the brain, in the sphere of intelligence higher and lower than yours, as well. Anipols are shared with animals and extraterrestrials. They have a wide breach hull, if you will, and a great berth of concept that you may share with creatures you deem so unlike you. So reach for the anipols when you need to communicate more effectively with that which you understand not, including your own commiseration. Anipols can never be completely destroyed, you see, in that they ride on nonmatter, and exist in spaces where space is not. They are facets of the truth. They hold in themselves tiny nuggets of truth, if you will, sparkles and remnants of meaning that will guard and keep your thoughts safe for a time. They convert regularly to accept what it is they must. They propel thought of every kind and shape and sort until it fits with a segment of another thought, until the match is made, for greater understanding. They operate much like a wrench and a nut, in that the match must be made before the bolt is turned. Anipols are God's gifts to you for greater understanding, not only intellectually, but for the arrival at truth and more truths to come. For they are ever changing in that they will arrest themselves in your time, you see, one after the other. When we speak of unyielding truths, eternal truths of God, we speak of anipols, facets, facts that have transcended time past the time barrier into the regions of All That Is. These are knowable in temporal existence, but they are saved to a different folder. And this folder will appear different outside your time. So the truths you hold here will yet change again as you are changed outside of time. These are the changeability I speak of, not to contradict what has been so beautifully said before in other texts, but to make you more aware of your condition as you stay here. It is blinded, and therefore, the use of anipols in the place of eternal truths, until you arrive at the place outside of this existence where you can truly see, feel, and experience eternal truth.

It occurred to me after receiving this session that the manufactured word *anipol* and its explanation as given above may help

explain how some people can communicate with animals. Also, when Simeon talks of our condition here as blinded and in need of anipols, he may be speaking about the energetic *klipah*, a kabbalistic term for the earth's metaphysical barriers to receiving and exchanging the full impact of Divine light. At any rate, Simeon declares that anipols are gifts from God for a greater understanding of All That Is.

Chapter Seven

Going On-Air

OCTOBER 19

A few days have transpired, and I am very tired tonight. During a transcontinental trip to visit friends—I feel much in need of a tune-up. So I will try for a few moments to see if anything comes across. I have a big day ahead of me, being a guest on WTTB 1490 talk radio, an hour-long interview about my early attempts at channeling Simeon Peter. Several meaningful clairaudient, clairsentient, and other empathetic experiences have occurred over the course of days, but I have not taken the time to channel Simeon.

It's not about me. It's about a love that blows down barriers between people. It's about a love that sings forward all that is and resonates within the souls of mankind. It is all that you find so difficult in your personal perception, what you judge and question and rightly so, while you walk this earth. What you wrongly judge and concern yourselves with is the chaff of your existence, you see. It is no more real than the source from which it came, which is your transmuted fear. And this fear transmutes from a place that you had not known before this place that you are now. To surrender this place in the now is the pathfinder for your souls. And what this means is, you will take yourselves outside of this time and space, the transmutation by the validity of your souls, which transcend space and time. And so in this, you see, you have found reason not to fear tomorrow, what may transpire tomorrow, or any other earth day you shall live. For you transmute through this time as well as outside of it. You are following a transition, a change, every day of your lives.

In the neck you must give attention to a lengthening and broadening for the essence to find my speech—and yes, it was earlier tonight in this strange frame of voice you nearly found me, although you were far from aware that it was I who would speak. The shoulder must find a source of repair. It has gone on too long. The map of what you must recognize in order to correct it will come forward shortly. In my predictions, you must understand, are contingent, too, upon your ability to trust. When the faith is not there, the time, as you see it, is lengthened. This is the only way to build upon what we do here, with the time and space you will need until you are ready.

And so for tomorrow, you have asked for a formula from me, and a way that you might speak with minimal repercussions, as it were, for what you might have to say. To avoid embarrassment, this is what you want. In order to avoid anything, what is it you must do? Do not go there in your thoughts. To focus on what I can [or can't] *give you would be a mistake. Focus instead on what comes forward in you, thoughts of the moment, and nothing more. In this you will stream beautifully and correctly and all those things you so desire. The ego comes from a very indefinite place because it knows no other way. Absolutism is not a definite place, either—it can be as ever insecure and supportive of the existence of the ego. So therefore, if you are to have wisdom, come instead from a place that allows beauty to flow where it will, for joy, love, and peace to go where they will, and do their good work.*

This passage about transmutation is a difficult one. Simeon seems to be saying that fear truly arises out of a nonreality, or nothing, and is transmuted, or given a higher form—among the many various forms—of fear, or fearful thinking. In order for fear to be useful, it must undergo further transmutation into love. Either way things might go, change happens.

Other channeling texts speak about the importance of spinal alignment, particularly in the cervical, or neck, region. Besides also affecting physical vocal patterns, neck alignment seems to have great impact on vocalization for the spirit realm.

The evening before the radio show, I was conversing with a local resident at a party that my friend, Helen Jessup-Murray, hosted for me. Mid-sentence, my voice turned hoarse, a frog in my throat, as it were—and attempting to clear my throat only seemed to make it worse. This went on for maybe twenty or thirty seconds. I continued talking in this odd voice, clearing my throat now and then to no avail. In *this strange form of voice*, as Simeon put it, were probably the building blocks for bringing him through vocally. At the time, I felt more secure with automatic typing, and continued in that manner.

OCTOBER 28

A week later as I read these words from Simeon—in light of what transpired during the radio show—which had turned out better than I'd expected—I realize the absolute wisdom in what Simeon had to say that evening in preparation for the show. It's been a busy week, and even with the need to sit for a session on my mind, I've also been preoccupied with my son's school. So I have missed almost ten days with Simeon. I'm receiving these notes on Sunday about 10:30 a.m.

It is imperative for this course of strain, the strain being the impact of words and thoughts upon the general public, as with any body of work, that you take the dictation as it comes for a while, until you find a better manner at hand for receiving that which I can give to you. It is of utmost importance that you stem from All That Is, as you have so graphically realized in the last few weeks. And the graph, in graphically, as you will understand it, is the network of lines that go behind open judgment, the field, as it were, the zero-point field, as your scientists are speaking of it at this time, before they will yet discover another way of viewing it altogether. This is coming in the next few months. A man by the name of Edgar, a doctor Edgar will be studying other phenomena at the time, and will stumble across this information. You may check this out on a website with mobility in its name.

For you to find this place of receiving me more clearly, you must adjust your neck more frequently for a time. I would not advise continuing over a long period of time, but just for a month or so. See if two- to three times a week will suffice. It is also true that this will assist you with shoulder pain you are experiencing. Learn to accept these adjustments from your husband, and you will find a way shortly to achieve them on your own.

I've never liked osteopathic manipulation of the neck, so for me to set out to receive these adjustments two- to three times a week seemed like pure punishment. My husband and I followed Simeon's advice to the letter, and, over a period of six weeks, the shoulder pain that had been with me for nearly two years was gone. The inflammation subsided, and I later discovered an effective method of self-adjustment that kept the neck and shoulder in stasis.

I frequently search the Internet for any breaking news or information regarding the quantum material Simeon discusses. The website http://www.endlesssearch.co.uk/science_wayofexplorer.htm seems to fit his description, with an article about quantum consciousness by Dr. Edgar Mitchell, the sixth man to walk on the moon. If not Dr. Edgar Mitchell, perhaps this is another scientist in the field of quantum study. It reflects what Simeon talks about in the previous session. Simeon continues:

The trap of anything in this lifetime as you know it is for one to become distilled in his or her viewpoints, and by distilled, I mean that which has no substance of change or expectancy of change. Change is the essence of All That Is, and in these changes we are finding our true selves, the very essence and nature of our souls. I am aware that I have emphasized this once already, and more, but the nature of the phenomena cannot be underestimated. It is the very reason replications do not really exist. Even in scientific replications, there is an element of transmutation and change that cannot be controlled, cloned, or otherwise. The reason I emphasize this phenomena so much, so frequently, is that in its essence, its plume, you see, is the very nature of existence and life. Also in its essence is the very nature of the attributes of God, and the impediments of mankind. For as you see anything impeding your progress from point A to point B, you will find this progress is not stunted, as you would believe it to be. It is merely a shift in focus for the moment, no more worthy or unworthy of your time and attention than anything else. Nothing is waste, my friend. Do not label things useless or unavoidable or any of the other nonsense negativity that mankind therewith chooses to name or categorize or label. It simply is, and is necessary for the transmutation to occur, which is always occurring, before our eyes and around our eyes. In other words, it happens regardless of our control or perceived lack of control. There are so many biological, chemical, and ethereal processes at work, it would be fast impossible to explain them in great detail for this text. Perhaps that can be reserved for another. But suffice to say that this indeed is the salvation of your soul, when you realize this neverending journey is first and foremost about discovering the transmutative affectations of your God. It is He—beginning, middle, end—Who set this into motion, without a beginning. For inside time, it is impossible to speak of some things. You must realize this. The words cannot be used as vehicles of description for what is out there, beyond the perimeters and barriers of time. Time is, in its essence, the transmutation of energies beyond the scope of reasoning alone. In order to accept time, you must be willing to suspend reason and live on this plane. I know this sounds ridiculous, but this is true. Your reasoning, the right reasoning of the whole Self is transmuted into a time-based existence with a reasoning and logic all its own. This is the factual data in A Course in Miracles. *It is true, and I will attest to its truth. So you may feel satisfied, comfortable once for all accepting what it has to say. We will add to it, as it were, and take away from it where necessary. By taking away, I do not mean an effort to disprove, but simply, a digression into what more it could have said, but for its purpose at that time, it did not. For in the essence of time alone, you will be finding and discovering many things as you go along in its history, and it lays out neatly from one moment to the next in your earth logic, for this is the only way you can understand its essence, for the most part, on this journey. The transcenders and speakers of your time and other periods of history have made a habit, if you will, of bucking up to time and all its constraints, realities, concerns, in saying that there is another way of seeing, and they question rightly so. For, as you have seen, there is, and there will be more to come, to convince you of the validity of the ergometric existence of non-time. That will be all for now.*

Simeon seems to be saying that even non-time can be measured by its energy output.

A few years ago when I first started meditating, I clairaudiently heard as I assumed the sukhasana (sitting cross-legged) position one day, "Sit here, Joliad." It later occurred to me that this could possibly be a whole entity name. This concurs with the idea that earth existences are personality splits of more complete and older souls that existed before any earth lifetime.

Science is defined in some texts as the art of right observation. A good scientific method requires that the scientist approach the task of discovery with freshness, curiosity, and skepticism. For scientific theory to become law, multiple replicated tests, or repeated experiments, are required. Simeon in essence is saying that nothing, no scientific experiment, can be replicated exactly.

Transcenders and speakers of ancient times mostly taught and spoke among illiterate societies and carried messages of a metaphysical order, which often challenged others to examine why they believed what they believed. Contemporary transcenders and speakers bring messages of the ancients, encouraging followers to develop untapped resources of intuition and examine why they believe what they believe.

ORDINARY OR EXTRAORDINARY?

NOVEMBER 2

Sometimes I am struck by the extremely ordinary nature of all this, this experience of sitting down and receiving this information that feels at times hardly different from the sensation of sitting down and typing altogether. I remember the first couple of days when I finally started receiving complete sentences from Simeon; I was happier than I'd been in awhile. I felt like I was walking on air. And so, it seems, I could soon start speaking for him in some fashion, or have that capability if I chose.

There is a part of me that marvels at these many things I've read about—the capacity to levitate, anomalously heal, bilocate, and others. But also I realize that there is a certain chemical construct behind releasing the ego—a certain formula, if you will, that can be reached over time in this plane—in order to do these things. Or at least, that is how I interpret what Simeon is saying until explained otherwise. So I will sit this Wednesday for another session, on the Mexican Day of the Dead.

You can see it another way, if you so choose. At any time on this plane, there are markers of intent that you will make as you walk this plane, for your business therewith, and for other phenomena with which you come into contact. There is difficulty, as always in explaining in your terms, but we will try. In the essence of All That Is, you have a barrier to time and space that all must cross when coming to your earth place, and in this barrier there is a transfiguration of all elements of matter and antimatter in essence, in order to reach your plane. In each matter and antimatter particle, substrates, as it were, there are neurons of proton, not merely protons of proton. And in each neuron, there are substrates, elements of core features in what must make contact with your earth. These are features which you contact every day, the solids in your atmosphere, as well as the gases that there exist.

I say this in order for you to understand that, to transcend these orders of your universe, and particularly your earthbound nature, you must will the ego to separate for a time from your presence. And the way to go about this partitioning of your self you have made is to simply set him apart from you with a simple or similar statement to "get thee behind me," or another [Mark 8:33]. *You see, it is reserved for devils of all sorts, including your self-imposed agendas of the ego. The ego sees and perceives this plane around you. Without it, you would not exist in this plane. It* [the ego] *is of a particular chemical configuration which allows you or anyone else to walk this earth for a time unimpeded by the proliferation of All That Is—all that exists around your earth plane. And so you would call this* [proliferation] *noise in your plane. Voices, sights, and feelings that are not congruent with what you deem at the present moment, or what is in your present moment.*

And so, the scholars of old, as well as the modern voices of your day so also rightly say that you must quiet and still the ego, sometimes with force, as in a shout for it to go behind, and sometimes by sidestepping what it would have you take in at the moment. And so all of these concerns that the ego concerns you with, let them go. There is—behave as if there is— no dinner to be made tonight, no hunger to be found, no child to care for, no schedule to be made, no job to be pursued, no next tick of the clock to be heard. Behave as if none of this is available to you now, and you will reach that eternal moment outside your time in which all these great things you have spoken of before can be found. It is a willful act on your part, and yet, it is a releasement of will—the will not to look upon this earth and its needs and wants it would impose upon you for a time. You must behave as if none of these things truly exist, and then for a brief time you will start finding a whole world outside of your own, and another existence, in which these things can be mastered. It will require more earth time on your part, and yet, it requires no time at all. These things are performed quite easily outside of time. Perhaps if you ask your dreams to become the impetus for all that we must do—simply ask, and add no more thought to it. Simply wish, and add no more longing. Simply strive only in the essence that you would have this with all your heart [reserve all the heart's space for receiving what you wish], *with no room left for the encroachment of the ego's desires, and what it would will you to be for the rest of your natural life. You are closing in now to a place where you will find your facilities more useful for doing and being that which you have desired. It can be an ego drive* [ego-driven, coming from an egotistical place], *to be sure. But as you take it* [become aware of and acknowledge] *that it must not come from the ego, as you recognize this, you will find that these things automatically occur for you, in essence, as these words are typed upon the page. We will let that be all for now. Sayonara.*

When Simeon speaks about *"not merely protons of proton,"* he may be talking about the proton-proton chain reaction, one of several fusion reactions in stars, or the conversion of hydrogen to helium. It is a dominant chain reaction found in stars the size of the sun or smaller.

Essentially, this chain reaction keeps the sun from exhausting its hydrogen supply and burning up. Proton-proton reaction was the basic principle of a theory about how the sun burns that was proposed in the 1920s. Following the development of quantum mechanics, scientists discovered that the tunneling of the wave functions of the protons through a repulsive barrier allowed for fusion at a lower temperature.

If the ego is substantially weakened, a person may well begin to experience ". . . *a proliferation of All That Is . . . voices, sights, and feelings that are not congruent . . .*" in life on this earth plane. Experiences involving levitation, anomalous healing, and bilocation would also potentially occur. For most people this would not happen accidentally or incidentally, however, but with much discipline and effort.

Chapter Eight

Conflict and Resolution

NOVEMBER 8

Our intuitive group met tonight. At home later as I dropped off to sleep, I entered into a state and sense of being everywhere at once, with a thousand visions passing before my eyes. In some terminology it might've been called out-of-body, but I sensed this corresponded with what Simeon described in the last session—stepping outside of the perception of real-time experience.

The site is finally shaping up to be something that looks and functions like a website. I sense that Simeon is pleased, and I do believe that some parts of it have come together much more rapidly with his assistance. I'm not sure where we're going to take it from here, but I appreciate more and more Simeon's attribution of "we," and I am more clearly understanding that the process of receiving these words becomes much more than just him or me. It is an effort of many.

I've still refrained from asking my 1001 questions of him, and I've also missed reading; too much focus on trying to get the site functional and continuing on schedule with my son's homeschooling. My work schedule has fallen into a pattern such that every other week I have clients daily. So life is busy, yet I continue to find time, it seems, to allow certain interpersonal conflicts to haunt me. I am curious why it seems mankind as a whole can't stop making or, at the very least, finding interpersonal conflicts, and how very difficult it can be to forgive oneself once they are made. So in light of what I've brought forward today, it will be interesting to see which direction Simeon heads.

A couple of that which you have aforementioned is worthy of time, and I will bring forward that which I feel will be of the utmost relevance for you as you traverse this plane altogether. This is for the others, as well. And so you have mentioned earlier that you will find it still difficult to trust that all your interactions with others work together for good, that all will absolve into something altogether strangely different than what you have experienced, you see. This is the nature of the chemistry with which you are taking this life down [transcribing], *as if notes, you see, taking it down* [transcribing it] *one chapter at a time. In essence you are forced to take it down in this manner, with one confrontation, or affront, following the other, a train of experiences, you see, and a runaway train in fact, for many, in that you would never cease to look for the reasons that it impetuously comes forward into your existence. You forget the elements of attraction for which you are so fond of dealing—in essence, your attraction of All That Is is the reason for all that is. Now I can hear you say already, question rightly, that this would place the essence of God into another category altogether in your minds; it does not have to—it is not necessarily so. The essence of God is one of all knowing, to be sure, but is also one of all sharing. And so, you may take that which*

He has shared with you and share it with another, you see. This multilevel sharing is the existence which you know and understand now, and sharing on this plane is disrupted by the elements of chance, change, vicissitude with which you share here, that the ego would find it difficult to share without the essence of letting go and so, the masters, the texts, emphasize the nature of letting go—this is for the ego, you see—not written for the spirit. For the spirit, the Higher Self, has never in essence attached itself in the first place—it is in a primordial state of having let go long before it has arrived. And so, you see, the nature of all that you deem conflicts, human conflicts in this earth plane. They are not real in the essence of spirit [the Higher Self]. *They have not occurred in the same way that you understand them here, how you understand they are occurring, in essence, from the time you first set foot on this earth until death, this is only in the state of being with which the ego has found itself. The chemistry of the ego and the conflict, if you will, in which it operates, is in this substrate we call time. Time and space are substrates of a reality far greater. And so, I have repeated these words I choose to use on several occasions, and this does not diminish their meaning to the reader. These are the terms with which I choose to express myself because these terms are not easily misunderstood. They are of a nature that all men may translate and fully understand once they have laid them forward one by one. And the repetition is necessary in order that the consistency of the nature of what I must say come forward. Essence, for example, is a very useful word in describing the nature of something. We could further subdivide* essence *into millions of particles, matter, and antimatter, to be sure. And so it serves as a useful word, and will be repeated many times. It does not negate that I am the one who is speaking.*

For the power of human conflict to exist, and keep on existing, you must understand that a man wills what he wills out of a nature, an essence he has been given while he traverses this earth plane. It is no more necessary that he rule his thoughts by this essence, that he rule them by his spirit, or another essence of sort. But it is given him in order to traverse where he may in the nature of these elements. And so, I will digress to say that he will never find the pallor of what he is doing until he is finished. He may suffer greatly, or believe he suffers greatly, but the pallor with which he sees his deeds is not the [total] function of his essence here, or in any other plane. He sees what he must focus [on] here for a time, and then he is gone with his pallor left behind him, for others to take up. The chain of events, as it were, is the reality in which you find yourselves living. And it must be borne for a time, it is a burden borne to be sure, when viewed in one way, as it is the necessary chemical construction of all that is to be had, in another. And so, I cannot offer you much comfort in these words of late, but I can say this: in time, you will find a construct of thought and space and existence that is far more than you have dreamed and hoped and wished for, and it is the nature of all-knowing, or the great bird's-eye-God's-eye view with which you have acquainted yourself, and in this construct you will stand outside of yourself and see the truth. And in this truth, you will fully understand all that I have spoken, and all that any have spoken, concerning human conflict and its possible resolution. For without time as a construct, you see, resolution and conflict are inseparable. Amen.

I asked Simeon if he had any instructions or directions for the site. He responded, *Forward one part to another website that I will reveal to you shortly.*

NOVEMBER 14

I've turned from obsessing on launching the site with all its difficulties and corrections to returning health to my son's new guinea pig, Relay. He is in respiratory distress, although his symptoms for congestion, heart murmur, and accompanying signs that go with respiratory distress are for the most part absent. Perhaps this is the day's enlightenment: the ego constantly seeks for something to trouble itself with, or to obsess on, or at least mine seems to do so.

My husband is not one to obsess like me, but even he carries his own load recently, finding himself embroiled in hospital politics. I've decided not to directly ask Simeon concerning any of these manners, as I see his wisdom is a sum-total message that transcends even every obsession that comes our way.

There is an element of foreplay in everything you must do, and in this foreplay what I am speaking of is the essence, once more, of taking on and tacking on events in your thoughts to their rightful ownership, you see, before the act of commission is transpired. In this foreplay you will often find an obsessing nature, the back and forth of the mind between its various constituents of thought and possible actions, probability of outcome, if you will, if one action is taken over the other. It is only human nature, it is what it is, to take each of these moments in foreplay with brooding and obsessing overtones, you see. For with what you concern yourselves is the stuff of God, no less, it is the playing out of all creation, as you are a part of it. So it is worthy of your foreplay, your obsessions, your thought, your what-if games, your trials and tribulations, if you will. For in these you are making the outworking of your souls. You are living out the very fiber of your nature; you are constructing the very fiber of your being to come. Yes, you are changeless, in one sense, but changeable in another. God has given you this freedom of choice and creation and becoming. God has also given you the nature of your Being, your Highest Self, to concur all that you would do on this earth plane. The growth you receive here is never worthy of more than it can make in this lifetime—it awaits another time and space after its being is tarnished and taken from this plane. Though this may seem contradictory to things I have said, it is not. It is the nature of the elements in which you immerse yourself as you pass through this plane. But remember this: you are just passing through. The elements with which you tarnish your creative self, the one that you made, will not last beyond this dimension. You again will choose to create another self with a lowercase S to traverse this plane if you so choose. In it are lessons and corrections and new assumptions of thought that you cannot encounter otherwise. For once you step outside of this plane, you step into the plane, the dimension of total truth. There many things are understood that you were veiled from receiving while walking here on earth.

The challenge of any business of this nature is to see with the eyes that eternity brings down to this plane. This is the focus with which you should make up your existence, you see, for even as you are making it up as you go along—do not be convinced that it is otherwise. Within the perimeters of eternal knowing, universal knowledge, foreknowing, the moment in time, you see, there is this endless creativity that can take place within planes like the earth, that are formatted, so to speak, inside a time-space continuum.

HUMAN CONFLICT

I thought Simeon was finished. Then a flurry of words burst forward. I typed at breakneck speed.

You may take this down as coming from your own source, or you may speak of it as coming from another who is not you. That is up to you. Now for the people of the hospital, I shall say this:

To divide and conquer was a resource of war in the Middle Ages, disseminated at that time from Genghis Khan, which proved to be a resourceful venue in that era of warfare for the global expansion of mankind and its civilizations. However, to divide anything requires a thorough knowledge of the effect on its substrates, and that, you do not have. The substrates that engineer and manage this hospital are ones that run on a delicate balance, from life to life, employee to employee, manager to manager, and who are you, or anyone, to upset this delicate balance? It requires so much more than a contract, so much more than the nature of which you concern yourselves with at this moment. It is not a piece of paper, it is not a set of legal stipulations, it is not a man or a woman who comes to work and punches the clock—it is all that and more, the very destiny of your souls here that you tinker with. You have no knowledge of how this earth will exist ten years from now, and yet you do. It is hidden deep within the recesses of each of your minds, and you could tap into it any second if you so desired. But many of you will not attempt to do this because of various religious beliefs and taboo inherent in this Western culture and society. So you mutter and moan over a contract, over money, over the stability of an entity in which you toil and labor to find a happy meeting place, but I will tell you, with this view that you take, as you segregate and separate each of its essential resources, there is none. It functions as a whole, as a unity, and there is not one jot or tittle [Matt:5:18] in life, not one breath that you take, not one turn of a pencil or stroke of a keyboard, not one mistake or error that you find, correct, or don't correct—not any one of these is without its meaning in your existence, and it all resides on a balance so delicate, that to try to separate or skew, toy or tinker with such a blessing of balance, you see, to try to reach with an overarching power play to control each of the individual ticking parts is your gravest error, and one that cannot be compensated for. So I would encourage you to spawn only that in a day's time of which you feel worthy of the cause, to pray without ceasing, to walk the course of this earth with a measured and calculative advantage, and this is it: to take each day as it comes, mistakes and corrections, highs and lows—and realize that in many circumstances, it is what it is. But that which is in your power to strain through the cheesecloth, to separate the wheat from the chaff, if it is in your doing to transmit kindness to another living creature as you would to yourself, then let this be, and do so with gladness. And if you cannot do this, then this is your signal that something is terribly amiss in your thinking of why you are here this day in this life, and you should reflect a moment, or even several—about why we are here, why this unity in contagion of action is so necessary for your continued existence. This delicate balance is obstructed with the myriad emotions of fear—and fear has many faces. You should acquaint yourselves with them well, for they will never give you the balance you seek. The disruption of your thought process by fear or any emotion under its disguise is the heartbeat of all things destructive and damaging in your plane. And yet, even in this meeting, it is not without reason to say that each of you here stands at a gateway of decisions that will affect even the outermost parts of the earth. It is not a stretch you see, to say this, that all your thoughts and your actions shape this universe, moment by moment and second by second. Nothing you do holds insignificance as its dinner. You are cooking and concocting the stuff that this universe is made of. Be sure of that. Divine ordination carries within it human intervention, and while your religious beliefs may concur that I am incorrect, simply look at your outworking in this world and see.

THE END OF SEPARATION

At the time, I was in no way prepared to read that kind of statement before a general public, particularly an antagonistic general public. I read it to my husband "for his eyes only" and wondered why I'd received it in the first place. Was I supposed to deliver it? Was I supposed to keep my mouth shut? Was Simeon's message only for me and my husband? Simeon comments below.

NOVEMBER 15

To care deeply regarding any situation is to make of it what you must. You are the stuff of its concocting in that you fuse yourself with the very essence of its nature, even chemically so. In that you must take down these words, you are so concocting your future, as well. It is still difficult, I know, for you to feel that you have attained them rightly so, but you indeed have. Goofs and gaffs come with every form of transcribing, and you can be sure you have it right if you will take a moment before each task and weather yourself, that is, season yourself for the task at hand. This involves taking on some of the elements with which you will toy with during the conversation. By toy, I do not mean to decrease its seriousness, or the very nature of what you must transcribe. It is simply that in its diction, it is a toy, it is a vehicle of play for the moment. It should be approached with the joy of play, even in the seriousness of its intent. For in this toying with your reasoning, you see, I transmit the joy of God. The joy of God, the anger of God, are one. It shows all sides to you at once when you take this down as I unfold it. These matters are not easy to speak of in your language or your time frame, but we must. As we go along further, you will see more of what I shall bring forward about this nature of God's joy.

As far as what you choose to say concerning the hospital, it's up to you. The words have been spoken. You have reread them and made necessary corrections [typos] *for this time. In their nature, they will address many concerns, though they may as well open up many more. Frugality is one approach with which I am not acquainted. Yet it is not in my nature to mince about with what I deem to say. It is within your nature to pore over what it is that you must say and do, and as we have discussed, rightfully so. I am shielded from the nature of what you must do, or so you should think. In this shield are common threads of instrumental belonging, however, as we are of the one whole. The separation causes much confusion. You have a right to know. The separation in its causal effects will continue herewith as long as you observe them. When you further split separation and its contents, you will see, however, that none* [no separation] *exists.*

Causal statements are not necessary. There is no need to give cause for this reasoning at hand. It came from deep within. The real work in this will be to make an effort to attend continuing hospital meetings. The rest will come naturally.

I never spoke publicly at any of the ongoing hospital meetings. However, Simeon prepared me to do so.

A proper introduction:

I would like to read a statement from a gentleman who could not be with us tonight. He is a minister, and I believe his words speak with a clarity I have not heard for some time.

Then Simeon closed the session with this statement. I thought often about how differently my life would evolve if I daily took its principles to heart without faltering.

Rely on nothing that you would not find comforting to your utmost blessing of thought. Quietly proceed with your soul exposed only in the sense that you bare it from joy. Do not ponder today too much. Allow it to happen as it will.

Chapter Nine

Divine Light

Although I will always have many questions, I approach today with no agenda for Simeon Peter. Let come what may.

And so, for you to continue in this way and further out, you will see that in the intimations of your soul, you will find me. Pay particular attention to the word intimation, for it is ever as real as the next word you shall receive. It is faint, or shallow at times, you will see, and at others, it comes rushing forth with all that you can or will ever receive in utmost confidence. So do not fret any longer that you should not receive from me while you apply yourself to the task at will. For in the will are places of eternity, you see, places of God, places which God has put in your heart for doing His good work. In the levels of the mind there are struts for each of these developments you must make as you go along. And in these struts you will find that the elements of development are not entirely the same, they procrastinate a bit for your eminence [from emanate, to radiate] to call forth, the eminence of which I speak is that which all men carry, the light of their souls. In some this light has been fast near put out, to be sure, in that these men do not operate from a place of light, but darkness instead. And that is the toil of this earth in times that you have known and will know. And so, to these men of darkness, who cannot let their God-light shine or will not let their God-light shine, it is for a minuscule, infinitesimal moment that they should turn back—and in that moment, if they would will themselves a kind word, even in that brevity of time, they would spare the light of their souls. The light is never lost—it is merely moved. And to spare it, you see, is to put it back in its rightful place. The sparing of light in souls to come, this hearkens to all that is so integral in making the world of a fashion in which you will live on in harmony and peace with God and man. It is not impossible, and yet, in the course of time, it seems so very impossible. This is what Jesus meant when he said, "Greater are ye than this, if ye will but placate your souls in the moment that they should stray from the truth of All That Is." Plunder the soul, and you will be left with nothing. But to placate, to satisfy the soul with All That Is, of which it yearns for, this is the measure with which you will find your greatest end indeed. Amen.

Come forward with all that you are into a space of fervent platitudes. You will see. That is all for now.

THE SUBSTRUCTURES

NOVEMBER 25

Thanksgiving was, as it always seems to be these days, its mixture of ups and downs. I carried with me thoughts from *A Course in Miracles,* intentions to forgive all the errors my ego sees around me.

I hoped to be a responsible catalyst.

At the same time, I do not see how I can continue to meet with my extended family in the same way. There is a strong urge to simply insulate my immediate family—to go away and make our own holiday. After much thought I am no closer to an answer. Perhaps Simeon will have something to say on this.

Fortitude comes with an approach to life that no other surface structure can offer. In this strength you will find that you do not venture far from whence you came, in all reality. From whence you came is the personhood of God, the substructure of your very souls. In your heart you know what is right for all concerned, but in your mind, you are split in two. For with each and every member that exists in this substructure of souls, you see, you view them separate and incomplete. And so you may only see them as incomplete in this earth plane. For to do so requires the eye to survey the populace of mankind in its essence of fortitude only in a minute quantity of who they really are. This is not the fortitude of God. The fortitude of the ego souls that you have created, the ego section of your minds, is what often guides you in your day-to-day decisions of such and of late. And thus, you find yourselves at cross-purposes with yourselves. For you are never enough in the ego state. You are sorely incomplete and fractured, chastised and scorned. It is never enough. There is always error, always wrong, only insignificance in this state of being. The ego knows no other way.

For you to rectify wrongs, to challenge that which threatens the ego from within and without, you must do and choose this: you are any day and every day, God's child. That is not to be forgotten. It is the true essence of your soul and anyone's soul. Overlying this true essence are layers of deceit, the masterminds of what we think we must do, or feel we must do, to continue on in this world. There is no plan that will guarantee you escape from all that you have made. And so you may adjust and shift, here and there, but nothing can replace the correction of your perception through forgiveness. You will wait for a time, and see that this is so. For in that you have studied it greatly, you have not mastered it. This correction is something to be mastered over time, and time again. It is a series of life journeys, if you will. It is a series of understandings, that these things that you have made do not really matter. There are worlds outside your own in which you subsist with this one, and those worlds are the essence of your true souls. In those atmospheres you take with you all that is given from God, and you use it rightly. You use it well. You are not impeded by ego in the same way. The substructure of your soul, which is God's, is there free to roam and be what it can be in any given moment in time, and yet where there is no time. In this timelessness, you find the eternity of your souls. It was always thus in God's plan for mankind, you see.

I asked for more clarity and details about human interactions, perhaps something I might use in my own interactions with my extended family, about how to bring them comfortably together again during the holidays, without splitting into factions.

There is nothing you can do or say that will shatter the

substructures. They are what they are. The souls you encounter are and have been so molded into their environments that they have made, so it is difficult to provide a blanket format. But I will try.

To all members of my family:

You are the reason, within each of yourselves, that we continue this tradition called Thanksgiving and Christmas; that is, you become the gatherings within themselves. You are the substructure of why these holidays exist. In every way, you are the foundation of what we have that is ours. That said, the undergirding of this foundation that we know and have cannot rest upon human lives alone. It cannot stand upon all that you see before you in material circumstance. It does not dwell in a house, or houses; it does not meet within the substructure of a building or meeting place. It meets with first our souls. They are the substructures of God, or knowing Him, and of sharing Him. And in Him alone are we free to be the families we would desire to be. My heart has been rent a few times because I have not sensed the closeness that the love of God can provide with us. It transcends religious preferences and it transcends any difficulty that man will make. So I call out to all of you to allow God's love to transcend all barriers you erect in your lives against His sons, which is you, my family. You are the sons of God in every way as much as Jesus. We are called to behave as sons regardless of the fold in our commitment to one another. What I mean by this fold in commitment is the place in which we feel things are no longer working. I have reached this place several times in the past few years, feeling that I should separate my immediate family and go our own way. I have even tried this. But I know that this is not the ultimate answer to all that bewails any family tradition. We must rise above the traditionalism if we are to continue as a family unit. It is my pledge to continue to seek God with all my heart. This is a pledge I made before coming to this earth. It took me a while to realize this, but the real me was all that God had given to me from the very start, which included an immense desire to know Him through all my relationships, one to another. In this God we all can see each other as marvelous extensions of all that He is, and not the egos with which we merely seek to survive. The ego, in the sense that I understand it, is the nature within all of us to view things inside a box, to insulate, to feel that we are being attacked from without. But who can truly attack the sons of God and succeed? That is the eternal question. As it plays out before our eyes we may believe we are the conquered. But this is not so. We are victorious in Him every day. Go and see for yourself.

So, in spite of my tendency to wish to become a catalyst for separation, for discontinuing the tradition as we have known it, I call to each of you to find a way to make this part of your lives work better. To overcome all that separates us. To truly join in prayer, and a single prayer, as prayed by the apostle Peter before his crucifixion:

> ***Pity and penance*** *are unnecessary for me to enter Your space, O Holy One. I hang here in defiance of all that I would become should Your tender mercies be laid aside. Receive my soul in the comfort of Your arms; in the fold of Your heart alone do I seek refuge from the storms without and within. In the Most Holy Presence I will place my soul forever, on this day and without end. Amen.*

Simeon ended the letter with the prayer above and gave some personal footnotes to me:

The state of any union must transgress its own boundaries in order to be effectual as a working unit. One must know when and how to alter its course in order for it to work with efficiency and efficacy. And so I will say once more, that in this soirée with your cousins and the rest, you must turn within to the voice for God, and allow the Holy Spirit to speak more fully to your soul. It is a tendency of yours to take out things piece by piece, to dissect all that is, and hope for answers from the pieces. The answer always comes from the whole interaction, the interaction of the whole. Do not forget this. Always, always seek to find the bigger picture. From life to life, generation to generation, and then you will understand the reasons for the interactions, the individual courses of action of your various lives one by one. Look to the whole and you will understand its parts. You will never understand the whole by looking at its parts. The substrates are part of an amalgam of substructures that transcend all its parts. This, and always. Amen.

HEAVEN AND HELL

DECEMBER 2

It's already been a week, and I've been busy with the site, even considering how to restructure it over time. I helped a friend with her computer, dove into more schoolwork requirements with my son, and came down with a cold. So there have been many things that have prevented me from coming out for a session.

I'd like to say I come out with no agenda, but I realize that in this reality there is always personal agenda—the day's schedule, how Simeon will be received, what to eat for lunch, my husband's ongoing medical politics, my son's school. Also, a couple of friends asked for readings from Simeon. These readings involved answering by e-mail some of those perplexing life questions, so I wanted to allow extra time for them. So while I'd like to come as an empty slate, I realize that this never truly happens. Even my dreams seem to have wrapped within them some precognitive information about spiritual lessons I'm about to experience each day.

For they are willing, in a sense to come forward one by one, if you will allow them in the mercy of all your souls, that which you have received from God. And in this reception, it is a receiving of one to another, not in the reverse, for it can never be a reception in the sense that you know it in the here and now. It is not a gift, but recognition of a fact that already exists. You will share this with many, but few will truly receive. And so, we must continue now.

In the beginning, when you first started hearing me, you were concerned about the correctness of the meaning of all that you would receive, word for word, and I know that your confusion still remains somewhat, so, I will be perfectly clear: For it is not which you would receive, but what you already have inside you—this is the outworking of all that has always existed, period. For what I may say over the course of time in essence will not change, though the words may be different, or the same. You are receiving what is and was and always has been. Amen.

And so, with all that meets you these days, you fret that I might involve these sessions with an ego-based phenomena and fail to give you something better. And I say, it will involve both. You can have the two without, and the one. And so, let us proceed.

For a time you will see that the words I give will have less meaning than not, for we will explore new territory, new ground, uncharted waters, if you will. So fret not. It will all become clear as we go.

Should you feel the need to persevere in another way for a time, it is for you to decide.

Countless lives have been involved with getting and giving as you would suppose it must be in this world of give and take, and more of the latter, if I must say, is often perceived by men whose souls are run by only what they perceive as good or evil. But there is more, between these substrates, the amalgam of all things that have ever existed can be formed and fashioned into a tiny dot, if God so desired, you see. But His desire does not override yours, and thus, we have the expansion of the universe and the galaxies and universes beyond. And so, you must persevere beyond the dot, although you can realize that at any given point in time, it can all be reduced into a size where it doesn't exist, into this tiny dot of existence.

And so you will take God's preparations for any future, you see, and fashion it after your own somewhat, and another's and another's and another's, and so on—a chain reaction of purpose and agenda and destiny. And so, it is, and always will be. On the one hand you say, "But how? Isn't there a Heaven beyond where such torture no longer exists?" *That is the conventional means of viewing what it means to embrace the earth, then leave it forever to the eternal beyond. But this is not so. You make Heaven first in your hearts, and as you extend*

*yourself to all that God has available for you already. As you recognize
the will of God in everything you do, and behave as if it were so
[should you fail to fully believe or accept it], you will see. Heaven is
where the heart is, and a heart after God's daily will not be
disappointed. But it is not an easy escape to pass from this dimension
to the next. It is not a street paved with rubies and jewels and gold. It is
not an essence too far from what you encounter on this earth plane, in
that you are still the choosers of your souls' destinies. You will still
make a friend as well as an enemy, but in the planes beyond earth, the
amalgams are different, changed. And so you will find new ways of
making friends and enemies, with less need for the latter. And so this
warfare in the beyond, it reeks of nothing like your own, but is in
essence a warfare in its own right. Although it may merely be a battle
of energy, of chemical substrates too complex to allow here, it is
nonetheless a clashing of incompatible kinds.*

*I say this not to discourage you, but to encourage you that
Heaven and Hell are not so finely separated as we would have them be.
They both exist in all parts and all spaces. When you remove the
spaces and go to dimensions without them, you will finally understand
their congruency in keeping All That Is in existence, if you will. The
Chinese are not far from making this a truth of all time. It is a truth in
essence as they see it, but one that more likely exists out of this
dimension than within it.*

Simeon's apparently contradictory statement in the previous
session " . . . *you fret that I might involve these sessions with an ego-*

based phenomena and fail to give you something better. And I say, it will involve both. You can have the two without, and the one . . . " always bothered me. Hadn't he taught throughout the text that the ego was a detrimental part of humanity? Something to be fought, stripped of its presence, or at the very least, sidestepped or ignored? Now he appears to be embracing it!

A wise teacher once said, "You also have the ego to help you safely field traffic as you cross the street, in order that your consciousness can experience earthly existence long enough to transcend its form." At the heart of this and Simeon's message is that the survival mechanisms of the ego are bound up in every undertaking we have on earth. In this way, does the ego become an instrumental part of transcending itself? *Course* purists say no, that the ego merely convinces the mind for a time that it is capable of preserving life in the body, but it soon becomes self-evident that this, too, will not last indefinitely. Proponents of the *Course* regard the ego and the human physical form that houses the ego as illusion, with the Higher Self being the only reality, and the only reality that is one with God.

Which begets the question: why then, do we need to experience the illusion? Simeon's teachings seem to rest on the cusp of this subject matter.

While what I experience in this body, including the transmission of these words into written form, may be illusion—herein lies a paradox: that an illusive vehicle by transmitting words attempts by this transmission to communicate what it means to transcend form.

Words   may certainly capture some of what it means to

transcend form, but words do not accomplish the transcendence itself. I've often thought that perhaps we would experience no desire to transcend form if form weren't illusive—that form's illusion motivates a desire to transcend.

Chapter Ten

Solitude Versus Isolation

DECEMBER 7

I'm coming back after a pretty wicked cold.

In order for you to receive fully, you must await all that has come before and will come behind you. It is an ethereal situation in which I have not instructed you fully just yet. It will come over time, which you are not so fond of spending, but it will come over to you in a way that you cannot understand from books and magazines. So be prepared for it, and you shall see. To prepare yourself is to wait for a time longer than you have before now. In essence, all that which you have read of is taking his or her creativity, all at a moment's notice and throwing it out at your behest—and in these moments you find a glimmer of hope and peace, and courage to go on. And so, you must forthright go and see for yourself what this has come to mean in your life, and in others.

Solitude can be a place of overwhelming gratitude for its Master, a place where He can instruct, teach you of the way to Him, without the interruptions of the mind when going about a day's chore. Solitude is unnecessarily labeled many things, but know that it hearkens you from All That Is, each time you should choose to endure such isolation, as it were. Isolationism speaks from a different master, you see, isolation comes from a particularly negative arena of mind that sees itself as the only soul in travail, or in [seeking to create] *its own absence, it* [the soul] *hopes to find a quietude and rest that cannot be given. The difference between isolation and solitude is thus:*

For one to override the other is only a step or two from the ego. If the ego prevails, one is caught in a web of confusion about his or her existence in the world. Questioning is not confusion. To throw up questions is to receive answers. In this solitude and solitary confinement, if you will, the confinement is only necessary in that it gives a deepened sense of purpose. If the purpose is gotten, the deepened sense of reserve and significance of solitude has prevailed. If one comes away entrenched in the purposelessness of one's own fortitude and continuation in this earth, then isolation has encroached upon a perfectly good part.

The line is thin and narrow between the two, and even here the ego tries to ascertain its position in the soul, from which there is no place for it in the son of God. Rest assured. You may be tempted to make out a day of solitude to be isolationism, if your thoughts are sobering or even sad. But call back your soul within, and allow the Self to do its good work.

You have come far in a few months, and will again hold this conversation with me on a near weekly basis, for it is your struggle [as you have] *chosen to rise from a quagmire of unresolved hindrances in your past, and the difficulty lies in accepting what you are given over and over again. For in fortitude is peace. And in finding fortitude, is hope. To gain fortitude is to wander through the quagmire for a time, uncertain of this or that, in full understanding that you will find what you seek, and seek what you find.*

I think Simeon points out in the previous session that the thin line between egoistic isolationism and heavenly solitude is distinguished by allowing the Higher Self, or the God within, to call back the soul to its original purpose—regardless of the appearances of life's difficulties. This is the beginning of transcending the binding elements of this dimension.

THE CRUCIFIED PSYCHE

JANUARY 1

Since my last session on December 7, I've been busy or preoccupied. I'd intended, perhaps not intently enough, to ring in the New Year with a session. The most troubling of Simeon's discourses to me remains the very early one concerning Christ's escape from crucifixion, and I believe I'll have to let that one go for a time. I've also felt there was a specific reason, and one I shall discover yet, for Simeon posing that session so early. And so now, on January 1, I'll begin with this problem, but remaining generally open to whatever comes.

Impartation generally receives a core feeling that you have not yet mastered; this is the learning skill that is yet to come for you at a later time. In receiving by the pig, you see, it is charted before you what you have in common with this creature of choice, of focus, in its essence to sniff out its sustenance and its great courage to follow its nose. Its ears are there, too, reflecting that which your ears cannot [hear clearly] *in one reality, but can in another. For we must digress once more in all that I would speak to you on this day, and continue forthwith until you muster the courage that is innate in all pigs to sniff out its future meal. Forthwith is another way and you will rightfully see it when it makes its way to you; you do not have to seek for it much. It is there, coming your way already, in that you would desire to meet with me again. The break was necessary to undergird you with all that you will need in the coming days. Mark this, and recall it when it comes:*

For in as much as I would find it necessary to explain myself once again, I will speak concerning the Christ, this Jesus, and what the historical Jesus found in himself at that last moment, what he felt necessary to partake in at that last moment, in the garden, where he prayed. He was led down as is written, he was arrested, and yet, he was capable of escaping, passing through their midst. In the ninth hour of his captivity, we believe he did just that. And this Christ did not refuse or refute a responsibility toward the nature of man nor God, in his refusal to take upon him a sacrificial death by crucifixion, in its literal sense, you see. He took it upon him already in its spiritual and psychological sense.

You ask why he had to go into obscurity, why he could not continue to teach his disciples, to train others in his presence. He was, we believe, in a remote area somewhat north of Golgotha, living in caves thereafter. We have no written record of this existence, none.

We have only hearsay of those who saw him, here and there, scattered accounts about. For you see, if indeed it was he, he continued to use his powers of transcendence, the powers of eluding a man's grasp, or dematerializing at will, of cloaking, or invisibility to the very end. I am told, was told that he died in his fifties, perhaps around the age fifty-four, in reality. The statements you feel are necessary to obtain elsewhere, these will be provided in time. Christ is a multiplicity of forces about you, in one reality. And he lived, died, was buried, and transcended in another. This is the message he came here to teach, that all in another, we are him, and he is us. There is no necessary formula to receive what he dispels to offer.

Clarification comes in a switchboard in your mind; that is how I will describe it. It snaps from one essence to another, in its time frame which it elaborates, and in its beliefs that it holds dear. As you release some of these fast-held beliefs, you will find its efficiency will increase for all that I have to say and speak.

For Christ will come to you in an instant, at your bidding, in your receptivity, in your mind. And in human form, the Jesus we called Messiah knew all of this, and presented it to us on a daily basis.

We were excluded from his presence in material form only. We were allowed to commune with him in our minds, as we have written these discourses, and many that we have not included in the canon of late. He stumbled upon this way of teaching us, and while we held him dear in his material form, he knew that we would not move further in our transcendence if he remained physically among us. We were forced to grow, to receive the lessons of the body, in his physical absence. The material is only for a time, as he spoke, and demonstrated, among us.

The loss only matters to you, not me. There is no loss where I am. For you, it delays, but for me, it filters through in another fast [almost] *inexplicable way. We wait for another day, and continue therewith.*

To take this session, I'd waited for several minutes in a "childlike place," although Simeon had mentioned that this was no longer necessary. I felt it was important, in order to be able to receive this crucial information regarding Christ. Simeon seems to be answering from an earthbound stance regarding Christ's death, however, and unwilling to make any further clarifications about what he may now know about Christ's death other than the confusion he experienced on earth. I'm not sure why he chooses to answer this way, but I have a feeling this is not the last I will hear from Simeon about Christ.

When Simeon addresses me as the pig, I believe he is referring to the Chinese zodiac, that I am a boar, and to the boarlike characteristics that influence the way I approach channeling. Boars are generally very loyal to their search to uproot the truth. He also emphasizes that while I may feel or experience loss in missing several days or even weeks of sessions, he is not bound by the same sense of loss in time and space as I am.

OBSERVERS OR PARTICIPANTS?

JANUARY 5

I return on a Monday, no particular questions impending—only the desire to receive Simeon's words with confidence, with doubts removed.

Relinquish the weather of your spirit to another, and you will remain well. In another, the other is the one who remains with and entirely you throughout all time. The weather, as I am speaking of, is the soul encased in its rightful place, neither endangered nor in want of all that it feels it is not. It is completed in Him. It rests in Him. For in Him, it is all that it is in its entirety. Never less, and never more. It is completed.

For a day or so, you will expect more, and perhaps subside with less. It is a given, in the business you are up to, you see. There is no other way to receive all that you must go for; it is there, on the tip of your tongue always, and forevermore. Amen.

In a while you will come to understand greatly what I've been trying to show you still, and [with] more to come.

In the air are particles of mass that accumulate with time and over time in the distance, in order that you can understand what the distance should mean. In the distance, the vast space which you have created for yourselves in which to exist, are minute particles, or substrate called time and space, and they arrest for your beckoning and at your beckoning from day to day, remain at your beck and call, for more of them could come into essence for your strata (levels),even as you would wish them to be.

There, these are not fully developed into mass at the time of your reckoning, only substrates floating about in the pillar of this distance you call time and space, and in mass, they are not yet formed when they come into mass, they are indeed the stuff of which this world is made, but you see, they come into being at your beck and call, they are not [there] until you should chance to look upon them, and in this your scientists are right, when they allow for the transmission of, or the omission, of the observer. In text they are not in existence before the observer should calculate their fortune, and how they should come into being. En masse, when one or more persons should calculate and exaggerate the substrate into being, it becomes a planned and shared event. This can occur over millions of miles and minutes in your earth plane. And thus, mass events, mass telepathy, if you will, the acting out of these substrates over time and space, they vend and devend over the space structure which you make for them to pass through to your world which you observe in time. Devend is a word I use to describe the overture of what must take place as they allow themselves to pass into existence, into matter, in your time and space. Ovend would be to pass away, to pass out of this existence in your time. Devoid of these words there is nothing else to describe this transmission of matter, and therefore, I choose them to describe what I must.

Forward in time, therefore, is no more a reality than backward in time. They are one in the same, because they have been filtered through into your world and experience through the substrata [bedrock] *of your thought and choice. You are no more God in your thought than your brother is. Do not be confused into thinking that this makes you out as God, with overarching power to choose and create a world different than you see in an instant of time or space. It is much more complicated than that. But at its components, its nuts and bolts, it begins just this way. It does not give you* [power to] *rule any more than a single choice gives you rule. For in this viewpoint, that we choose our existence and therefore rule ourselves, we are sadly mistaken if we hold such power as even necessary—for the advantage we would take of one another, you see. The edge, the advantage we seek in doing so is already rescinded if we make such a choice in error and not truth. This is a difficult passage to impart. You may choose to wait, if you wish.*

Here Simeon concerns himself with the constituents of life, and just how many events are preordained versus evolving. In a sense that is difficult to understand, he says, human destiny involves both. Human beings are equally observers of, and participants in, reality. However, it is more complex than the two extremes, i.e. either we choose our destiny or we are victims of fate. I believe Simeon is describing how human destiny falls in-between participation and observation. Life, then, truly is a paradox.

JANUARY 18

We're in the process of moving to a different state, so many events have interrupted over the last few days. So, once again, I chose to wait a considerable amount of time. I'm sitting indoors for a session this morning, so we'll see how everything continues. I haven't been in the best of moods the past few days. Perhaps the best way to describe it is as a feeling of low-grade dread or a nagging premonition that something sad is about to take place.

In the present state of mankind, the one in which you subsist, you will find that the average man uses a figment [an illusion], *in another course or way of stating such, only that which he can release over time and space for all that he is to become while he cherishes his lifetime on earth. The figment, you see, is the lie that this state is his only reality, and it is a mere figment of all that he really is, regarding the multitudes of existences before and behind him. For he must come to recognize this figment in the territories in which he exists, and he will* [recognize this figment], *one by one, over these life spans he has created for himself. Some eras lend themselves more to his discovery of this figment he subsists with, and others, while offering it always in some places, do not reach him in the same way. And so he waits until another lifetime, in order to see that which will make the choices for him easier, in a sense.*

The lifetimes which you encounter, the memories thereof: you must know that the ethereal nature of the memories will encroach upon your minds regardless of your belief [for or against reincarnation] *in the existence of several lifetimes. In your approach to the many likes and dislikes of your personalities you will find the encroachment of other lifetimes, but this you do not recognize as such. In the meeting of one over the other, which often happens, the soul will transmigrate for a time to the plane where the other exists, and is existing, in your time frame, for you see, in these other spaces, time does not separate as it does in yours. A minute before is a minute after, and they are all one in the same.*

And so, for your curiosity concerning why the [reincarnational] *memories should be so very difficult to recall, I will offer this: they are difficult only in the sense that you may not recall them minute by minute as they occurred in your plane, for where they exist on the outset in other planes does not contain minutes, and yet they exist, simultaneously with the goings-on of your present day and current atomic time. And so, your difficulty in retaining memories is not a difficulty in retaining at all, but in maintaining a consistency within a plane that uses time, in conjunction with planes that do not use time.*

I find some consistency here between this and the previous session: a lesson concerning how matter comes into being—the energetic exchange, the passage, into space and time through *devend*—and the passage out of space and time through *ovend*. Next it seems natural to me that Simeon would address the nature of reincarnation and memory, and why we would have difficulty recalling memories of a "past-past" event, in terms of understanding past lives in linear fashion on this earth. These memories certainly can be recalled using hypnotherapy and other altered-state techniques, but remembering past lives is not the norm for many people. His explanation satisfies me that the difficulty in cataloging memories one after the other occurs because of the differences in dimensions, or planes. To pass out of time and space to a void where none exists, then back into time and space, would certainly seem to break the delicate circuitry of human memory as we know it in this time and space.

THE PURPOSE OF TIME

FEBRUARY 17

I've missed a few weeks. I'm inside this morning—it is cold out there, and the cabin is not sufficiently warm or conducive to deeper meditation. So, barring interruption, I will continue. I still have many questions, and I would like to receive some prayers that I could say on occasion.

The meeting ground of any continuum is forthright in a second chain marking. By this I intend to say that, given all circumstances, all events, all possibilities you are forever searching to the corners of antiquity in your minds. By this, you say and do all that you have heretofore given in fact, a way that you have made for yourselves a hundred times over, and yet you will make again. This is the nature of perchance in time. Things happening in your time, as the events unfold, you see, are no more happening in contagion than the sun rises before the moon. Which comes first? You see. Which was it, the sun or the moon? Therefore time has little meaning in the plethora of events and circumstances in which you find yourselves each day, week, month, or year. Time does not exist. And so, you ask, how is it then that we are still here, in this time, however? And I will say, that time has no consequence that you see, hear, taste, or feel—it is illusion, you have been beguiled from ages past, and so you go forward now in the same. Time is illusion, period. For you to exist at all matters not in time. It matters not in eternity. It simply is. For your ideas about what eternity is, while you exist in time, are distorted, as well. Time lends itself to distortion. And so, you ask, how does this come to pass? How can this be? We are each found in a segment we call time, at any given moment, breathing and living and loving and quarreling and dying in these moments we call time. They "exist" in the nature of our ego minds as we now carry them with us on this journey. But the journey neither starts nor ends. The mind stands above all—the Self mind, which you have made. But the ego mind stands in-between time and eternity. It points to one over the other. It perceives one, and distorts the other. In its perceptions are therefore more distortions at work.

And therefore I have not yet answered these questions concerning the nature of time, and I will call forth another way for explaining to inquiring minds. It is this: lay before you what you call time. Watch it go past. Recall what time has borne, what time has accomplished, what time has done. Recall all that has befallen you in this element we call time. Watch it pass some more. Then come back to me and tell me what you have learned in time. You will say, I have learned and experienced much on some days, and not so much on others. I will say, you are better for it; this is your purpose you have allotted yourselves in time, that you would walk the face of the earth with gratitude, with solitude, and in these moments, find that God is.

Although this session above was taken in a very light trance, there were a few interesting parallel thoughts in this discourse: the first being the parallel between the *non-journey* of the mind—that our existence *simply is*, and the second being the purpose of the non-journey to find that *God is*. I think Simeon is trying to say that while the time spent living does, for all intents and purposes, appear to be a life filled with lessons and journeys, that the reality is, we are already existing outside of that realm in a state that *is* with God. This is the "purpose" of our journey on earth—to find that we are not on a journey at all. Therefore, the closest earth experience we can parallel to what really *is,* is to quiet the mind and meditate on God—to feel the oneness and connection with Him that is and has always existed.

PRAYERS

We gather as one today for the purpose of drawing near to the God who surrounds us all in loving-kindness, in joy, in all the circumstances we employ in our journey in time. Whenever we stand outside of time with Him at last, we ask for nothing, because we know as part of All That Is, we have no want or need. For while we walk the face of this earth, we will only ask in its present moment what will provide our souls with strength and joy, and greater sense of purpose. That is our toil, our task, the ones we redeem from Thee. Amen.

Come before yourselves today in time and purpose, willingly serving first the essence of your souls. Give to yourselves that which has been given you—the hope, peace, and joy that you have received from All That Is. In purpose and in truth we will abide forever. Amen.

Let us pray. *Let us be one in thought and mind, as God intended from the days of antiquity, from the outskirts of time, from the inception of All That Is. Let us be free to share this oneness in glory, for that is the essence of All That Is. Let us be certain as we share in the One, that nothing separates us one from another, one from Thee. For it is, and always will be. Amen.*

Father, in your most tender mercies, *we stand before you now and forevermore. We come as one to partake, we come as one to exist as we are now. In each and every moment we pledge to be the essence of all we are, of all that we can be, and in this essence, we find joy, peace, and hope. Now, and forevermore. Amen.*

DIVINE BREATH

MARCH 2

In September of the previous year, my son and I practiced drawing portraits. While he'd worked on his own, I'd downloaded a bundle of baroque era prints, a conglomerate of features that reminded me of the young man I dreamt about on August 2. With a very rusty hand, I'd sketched a couple of portraits.

Now, months later, in our effort to pack, I threw away the early drawings and notes I made on Simeon's portrait yesterday, partly because I feel that his face is so carefully etched in the dream I had earlier, I will not forget. Also, I'll require some practice to complete the portrait I'm looking for. So perhaps, at a later date.

Biblical references to "The gates of Heaven," you must understand, were extracted from a course of time when all men used gates for various purposes. Gates were entryways into the city, posts for the public, punishment, a most froward, or [conversely] *hospitable, place for all men to shirk or shake what lay be fore them. You will see why I've used those words in the discourse to follow. Gates were entrances into our time, places of necessity to arrive at our own good or bad will, you see. Gates were the places of antipathy—the ropes of paradise, the pearls of Heaven, if so designed or disguised. (Sink a little more.) The matter of gates is and always will be the pastime of your souls, for you see, gates are the passageways of height at its best and shorn full of the moments in which the soul chooses to exist. Antimatter, if you will, is always an obstruction to the gates of the soul, in that it posts another solution and dilution of what is before us today. Antimatter is the antithesis of life as we understand it in this realm. However, the existence of antimatter is indeed very real and formidable in terms of its common state of being. You must understand that when we speak of such components of nature, these are the components in which the gateways will shore up their posture and wait for the signal. Upon the first burst of antimatter in that realm, there are funnels and passageways for it to travel, before it is carried through to other realms. These in themselves are gateways beyond your dimension. And so, the Biblical references to the gates, the eye of the needle, and others, you will see that it contains in part matter, in part antimatter, and in this realm of thinking, exacting the both, you will have rest for your souls. For then your thoughts fully comprise All That Is. Matter and non-matter, in its each existing passageway, travel to and fro along the nature of lives. And in these gateways, of which many exist in this realm—and in your own bodies, for they encapsulate in all forms of matter, down to the tiniest degree—in these gates, you will see, are the essence of life, and all life that is not tainted by factors beyond your control. To catch something at the gate, to clear the gate, in essence, is to present the soul with all it has and needs to accomplish anything it desires. So gateways are and always have been of utmost capacity to formulate anyone's existence. The existence is not merely in its whole of matter, but in the gates, the passageways.*

Passageways into incarnation are its entirety. When a force incarnates into another form, you see, its passage to that life is the gateway to existence. But it is more than just a matter of travel in its entirety. It is the heartbeat of all the essence of that matter, its personality, its drive, and its destiny. It is all rolled into one, and so therefore, preordination, in its essence, when one stands outside of time, is appropriate to deem necessary for the understanding of such events that seem "bound" to happen. It is the admixture of all the efforts and effects of passageways over time, and even outside of time, that a soul may travel. For souls go apart and together in many existences of your earth time and other places where time is a factor, but not in essence outside of time, in that nature. Souls culminate in other existences and it is not the same as the here and now. In eternity, where time is not, the souls, one would say, will find their happy meeting place, and yet, go beyond that realm of understanding that we all appear to have [here] *of what is happy and joyful. It is an existence that cannot be fully described to you while you are here. You can attempt to understand it in its parts, but you can never see the whole, as long as you shall live in the here and now. But suffice to say that in your companionship with your Maker, you will find the essence of frugality in all that is necessary for you to meet Him in the sky, so to speak. In essence, you are meeting Him constantly coming and going in this passageway you now call earthly life. You are not at all times aware of His essence, but suffice to say that each breath you draw contains Him, and so it shall be.*

If the hundreds of Biblical references to gates are interpreted energetically, the applicable meanings of these passages expand enormously. In the practices of Traditional Chinese Medicine and Qigong, a series of gates, or gateways, are identified as pathways to the body's chakras, or energetic systems. Among several possible energetic phenomena, chakra gates may become blocked or stuck open. The art of the breath, says Simeon, is the coming to a full awareness that something as seemingly simple and involuntary as breathing contains the essence of God.

PRAYER

We come to thank Thee for all that is laid before us today, Father, knowing also that in your essence you have designed more for us to acquaint ourselves with, far more, in your order of events that outlay all we have before us. Allow us to explore fully in this life, this essence, all that you would constrain us to be, and yet contained, we are not, for the universe is ours, as it is Yours, to extend and share together forever. Amen.

Chapter Eleven

The Nature of Eternity

With packing, preparing to move, and generally just spending time on some evenings vegetating in front of the tube, I haven't spoken with Simeon in several weeks. My laptop computer is in the shop, so I'm sitting for this session indoors at the mainframe. Given the hiatus and the location, I'm not really coming with any pressing questions or expectations.

Early in a stage of antipathy [ill will, opposition] *comes one or more sequences you have not forestalled* [prevented] *as of yet. In an instant, you see, eternity can be one in all and All in all. And such is time. For in a meeting of two hearts, souls, minds, in the moment of fusion as it were, you shall see a catching place for all things molecular in substance or frame or time frame. It will cover just about everything that has happened or can happen. In this substrate of time and presence you will find more still that will accord you with what another may not find as encapsulated* [easily summarized] *as you. It is for another you will wait and stay awhile; you must wait and try for a time, and the other will come.*

I sat for a few minutes afterward for a word on how to proceed with Simeon. I didn't want to sit at the computer or open my eyes in order to write notes. I was up for the challenge to try to receive an entire sentence, or more, clairaudiently by audible discourse versus mental streaming, but in order to do so, I felt like I needed to move away from the computer and just sit quietly. In order to receive this as being dictated audibly would possibly be much more time-consuming. This took several minutes for one sentence. There was some bleed through, but the sentence was slowly pieced together in linear order, and strongly and audibly clairaudient.

From your fingers [come] *a straight and open place where each one can inside find incredible comfort.*

SEE NO EVIL
APRIL 17

My computer's back! I'm out in the cabin again. I look forward to perhaps a longer session this evening. I'm feeling a little scattered tonight—not for any particular reason that I can identify.

A tendency toward former ways lies perpendicular to anyone's net result, when achievement is the goal, not the circumstance. [If achievement of any kind is the goal of one's actions, the left-brained response is to stair-step perpendicularly; that is, to constantly compare the past to the present and the present to the possible future.] *And for you to achieve in such state is fundamental to your strings-attached syndrome in living the earth values of your time and culture.* [This left-brained way of achievement is earthbound and built on ego projections.] *And therefore, publication is not so grave a concept anymore. Yours should be perpetrated with the calling of kindness toward any reader who would find these musings of rapport, affinity, and adage in which honesty and fortitude can be found.* [The reasons previously stated would be the ethical goal of publication.] *In the height of any amusement are the building blocks of joy, though clearly, not all is even kind.* [Base matter has the foundation of joy, and so does amusement, although not all amusement turns out to be kind.] *But the stratus of joy exists, even in the vilest of offenses to be judged in its own right as it sets aside the purpose of joy for all involved. Joy anew, in pretense, and in recompense, will not further find into that which it metes out in sequence apart from what it is intended to bring about. Therefore, when joy compensates for itself, it fails in its essence to be joy.* [This establishes how we might distinguish true joy from something that is not true joy.] *If it is for All and in all, then its relationship to all is true. If it holds one at expense of the other, if it metes out cruelty in any fashion for the sake of humor, then it has contrived itself to be that which it is not. Amusement and the building blocks it contains are only the perpetrators of the fundamentals of joy. In this example, I have attempted to provide for you an example of how amalgam can skew from precious to evil in a heartbeat, in this time, this plane. Therefore, rules and laws abound for greater understanding of how to mete out judgment for such deeds, or recompense. You start to fuse them, altogether later following the cause-and-effect nature of all necessary in acquainting you with this understanding of crime and its payment. Attitudes of such will reign eternal, if not for the grace of God in truth, you see. For He recompenses none when none can be seen. The seer sees what God would have them be. He translates the messages before others, that others, in turn, may compensate their lives in such a way pleasing to all. Hence, the salvation of the universe. For God sees you as you were, and always—as you were before time spliced your network in two halves, good and evil.* [This appears to be a brief explanation about how life's mixture of events and circumstances can skew from good to evil, as well as the laws of recompense in this plane, the fusing of judgment, the intervention of the grace of God, and the function of a seer.] *Therefore, be brave and forego all stalling of this project as you would not have the shape before you in the same way as you do now.*

PRECOGNITION

MAY 11

I included more bracketed statements in last session than ever. It seems the material is becoming increasingly complex. I wonder what will happen today.

Before you write further into this sequence, of note: to propel oneself into an action of any sort or kind in future circumstances requires a prime device, as this will garner and supply most issues you will forever foretaste. In hope, in mind, in fortitude will one muster all courage for the event in one's time. And so, with that I recompense [compensate] *only that you shall see more of me in the future, as you have not in the past.*

Foretelling, in a sense, is a wavelength of the future not yet passed. In the wavelength are particles of matter not yet extruded from their sequences, the mental sequences at hand. You must see these if you are to ride the waves of the future, to foretell. In a sense, to foretell is to line all probabilities into sequences, one on top of the other, and extract the most likely. But in its essence, it is far more—and as you shall learn, can be far less. What I am saying is that in this extraction, the forage you seek is not of muster or gain, but simply is to stand in its own right, until it comes to pass. So do not suffer in what you foresee: it is all of essence, or material, that all comes forth in time. It is of a knowing that, when you correlate and corrugate these things into one, that you stand before others as having it on the nose. In these events, you are the apt foreteller, you are trusted and believed. But know this: in every foretelling is a past, and in every past, a future, and they are one in the same outside of time. So, in essence, you are simply calling things as they are. But what of the illusion? It is so that you may know that within all of it, exists only God, and that His future is not bound at all by yours, for He has none. He simply is. And to resolve such issues as you transmute these issues and events through time is not your concern. You can and will exist in the illusion while standing outside of it, if you trust that God does the same. And so then, your receptivity will hold what it is that He would present through his Holy Spirit for you to garner and thrust forward before the world to see [by foretelling]. *And so it is.*

Go, and prosper.

THE MERCIES

MAY 14

I don't practice foretelling regularly or consider myself to be precognitively gifted, although I have admiration for those who are. Simeon's previous session remarks about the difficulty, I believe, with the egoistic nature of wanting to be accurate, and the burden of proof that lies with any form of precognition. When we place precognition in terms of time being illusion, precognition no longer exists. We know and see through the illusion of time.

Do not calculate too closely how this will come to pass, or another segment of your imagined works, in which you project out into the future, each minute, day, or hour. For in all that you would find 'twixt and 'tween these moments, you will find elsewhere, in a sense, in the sense that you formulate these things one by one in this time, but not so without it. So, in essence, time is your albatross for formulating, for being imprisoned to formulate these, one by one. In another [plane] *you will find that, in this other space you will find that, this formulation no longer works. It is not so. It is only "true" in your time and space, you see. It taxes many and frazzles the soul, while you remain here on earth, but it wastes no effort in eternity, the true eternity. And so, you worry and will these things into existence here, but you fret not in the longer version of life, the life that extends out from which you cannot fathom, and to which you cannot fathom. These are the hidden parts of the souls of mankind at their best, and often at their worst, and they all have place in the universe of God. It stills the mind to know that God indeed intended for all that is to be—the good, the bad—and I say that He fully intended the makers of these events to derive satisfaction out of their course. Where this went wrong, as you put it, is in the recognition of things unmerciful and exponential to that which God had ordained, and you, and another, and another, has seen this so, in your lives and lives before. What I am saying is simply that, in the hardened version of what we all must do, we see sin and the wretched living and dying. In the softened version, we see that which we want to see. In the true version, we see all that God has made, only what God has made, and we say that it is good. It only ceases to be good when we encase it with bad—the like of which you will never fully understand until you are outside of the doldrums of which you find yourself in lately. In a sense, you have found only bad in search for the good. Reverse the course. Find only good in search for the bad. The premonitions or evil omens of others are often based upon finding these things. However, in your search for the bad, when you find good, what has taken place is the surprise of the mercies of God. In His law, you see, you will not find what you are not searching for. It is so. How, then does this take place? It comes in a figment of imagination, outside your plane, that allows to you the mercy, the grace to receive that good which you thought not and that which you sought not. It bubbles through from time to time. In this law of attraction, it is unaccounted for as of yet, but I say to you that it is as true as it is unaccounted for. It is grace stored in segments outside your reality, but by the prayers and merciful acts of the sons of God. It is residual energy pockets that allow good to come to those who expect bad at times, a merciful act, a jackpot, a lottery, or some such state despite our disbelief. For God knows that the pull and doubts of the ego are incessantly strong. And so it is.*

I enjoyed Simeon's discourse about the mercies of God. The law of attraction, or *like attracts like*, teaches that we draw toward us that which is the focus of our repetitive thoughts and emotions. The mercies, I believe, are those seemingly serendipitous events of good fortune or blessing that occur in spite of a gloomy or troubled outlook.

MAY 27

Look at them without a care or concern for tomorrow; this is and was the watchword of those who came with you and before you. But what does this mean? In its essence is a caring and desiring for all that concerns itself with itself, you see, more in concerning yourself for yourself. But strike not in this concerning, strike not the flesh that forwards or hinders you in your progress toward all that is concerning you at this or that time. For the concerns of today will not be the concerns of tomorrow, in exactly the same way; they are changing— and transmigrating, even as we speak. And so, you see, what concerns oneself with itself for today will not aggrandize itself in the same soliloquy tomorrow. It is a different song and dance each day as we traverse time, expect of time, give back to time, and receive from time. In essence, you are cornering an aspect of yourself in this world and saying, "See, it is of utmost importance that I do not pay you heed of any kind, for you are not real." And it is so.

And so, concerns of every sort will flee, for time itself flees. Therefore, in this passage you call time and space, the interdimensions thereof will also flee. You can see them, however briefly fluttering by in this time-space continuum, but I say to you, that nothing in this essence we are fond of calling time and space will last. It is at best temporary and change-filled, until it is filled no more. For God exists within and without this vacuum you have created called space and time, and it is only that, a vacuum, to be absorbed within the mighty and pervasive, everlasting mind of God. So therefore, do not concern yourselves with yourselves. You are only passing through, in this time, space, and order. It becomes self-evident as the body grows old, dies, and decays. But beyond what seems self-evident you must know that it renders another type of circumstance altogether in that you will pass here from time to time. While it appears fleeting and worthless, it is not without its value. More on this later.

I think Simeon makes an important point regarding the emotional value we place upon circumstances, relationships, or objects with which we engage ourselves during this lifetime. Emotional balance is found when we acknowledge life's change-filled, fleeting nature while understanding that nothing we experience or encounter is purposeless or wasted in the greater scheme of life.

ALIENS AND SHAPESHIFTING

MAY 28

I'm receiving this session in the cabin. I've come back the last couple of sessions wondering how many ways Simeon will find to describe the nature of timelessness, the illusions we endure, or the abilities to transcend time and space.

Before the fall as you know it, mankind was fortuitous to find within himself all that he could be in the foretaste of God, you see, and in that, man was once endowed with all the mercies and substance he could allow into his Being, that form once from God. And to see that form, all he had to perceive, to do, was "element" himself so. It was in his mind, he simply transmigrated at will, or shapeshifted, if you will, from that form to another. It was all at his fingertips, much like what you do now [typing]. Simply one stroke of the key over the other made entirely different [words] worlds for him or her, you see, in the heavens as well as on earth. Now we speak of the fall with care, for, in its nature, in that nature, it isn't a fall from worthiness, as you would desire to perceive it so. It has not marred your nature in the event of time or space, as you believe it has. It has simply transmigrated you once again, if you will, into another state of being, and one entirely more static than the first. The aliens know more of this state than you do, or what you choose to refer to as alien in your culture. In reality, they are older forms of you, those existing for hundreds of thousands of years before your kind, and with their brain size, as you have recorded, inherent within that large cranium, is the superior functioning of one's ability to form these things we speak of, these alternate realities, and the ones parallel and interdimensional to your plane of being. However, you must understand that the cranium capacity is not one of great import to your culture; it is not unfettered of its own accord. It holds merely the substance of reality from one to another, but does not generate that reality, in essence. What generates reality from one moment to the next is a slipshod fashion of existence in which you find yourself invested at the moment; it is a constant tweaking and twinging of all mankind, shifting from one moment to the next, with myriad processes of change occurring that you are unaware of. So what at the onset appears so entirely static in your time and space is in reality a multitudinous plethora of matter in constant flux. It moves and swirls around you, while you, [are] blind to its existence, or how it shapes matter around you. The aliens have more of a technological ability to harness this process, and have done so, with apparent ease. But centuries of work at the drawing board have reamed this out, for it is a technology that further translates matter into another existence—what I am saying is, the technology itself forms interference with the process of [natural] shapeshifting, if you will.

If the shapeshifter is of one accord with himself, for himself, by himself, and with others, he recognizes that he is no more or no less in synchronicity with one and all. He simply changes at will, it seems— but in reality he makes his bed as carefully as the next one. In this process, his mind is of one accord with his God, however he may perceive Him to be, for he has found his peace and trust with All That Is, that the events in his day are happening, all for good reason, which lends him more so to trust in this process. He releases a figment of his mind to the imaginary process of being another first, and being elsewhere first. He goes there first in mind, in thought, endearing the process, loving it, placing it in highest regard, that this is what he entirely wills and wants at this moment, not preparing or thinking or fretting about the next [moment]. *It is for him in this moment, and that is all he concentrates upon. The next step is one of wishing well upon himself and others, and this is what it simply is. As a well-wisher, he takes and partakes of All That Is, because he intends only good to rise from what he wills. He does not confuse good with prosperity, abundance, or advantage one over the other. In his good, he makes a sequence of events forward that pass through mankind like a shadow, for the good of God, and he does not define the good so precisely as some of your religious texts do. He wills that the good of God bless the process; nothing less, and nothing more. In this, he asks for the truth to come forward in its essence that always was, and guard the process. The final step, and only step, that we observe in the process, is the shapeshift itself. In this transmigration of thought and matter, we remember that it first began, and ends, with thought. It is a hallowed reminder that we all change, regardless. However static our time here may seem, it is constantly shifting before our eyes, whether we notice or not. And so the lines of energy, as you have observed, are ones that shifter rides into another existence of form. To harness those lines of energy is to make the shift. They must surround you and lift you up, move you about, and carry you into this form. They will capitulate* [from one form to another] *in their shift if you allow them to do so. And that is it, my friend, and always, to simply allow these things to be.*

A couple of years before I began channeling Simeon, I was practicing meditation according to the ancient Chinese text *The Secret of the Golden Flower*. I began seeing what I then described as energy lines with vortexes moving quickly around the room, flooded with sparkling light. I noticed when these lines intersected solid matter, they seemed to sink into it, so that solid matter itself seemed to fluctuate ever so slightly behind these vortices.

AT A MOLECULAR LEVEL

MAY 29

I come back the next day out of sheer curiosity. Can Simeon explain yesterday's session to me at a molecular level?

Make a circle around yourself and we will go in. Inside are molecular structures of tome and space, vacancies, as well, that are part of all that surrounds you within and without. Tomes are of particular order in this universe, and not so elsewhere. Tomes are of such kind that they seek out their Maker, their origin, again and again. Moleculars: p54 in particum sulfide plus one neuromatic peptide minus alpha particum partite. Genus: mankind. You know it well. Repeat: p54 minus alpha particum partite. The peptide holds your substance in existence, one chain of it only. Many chains appear, but one altogether holds you into existence as flesh and blood. Remove that chain, and poof, *you are gone. The nature of shapeshifting is found here, but with manipulation, versus removal of, the peptide.*

Peptide 46a in harmony with p54, b and c, will cause neuro matter to rot. Now, before I confuse you further, you must understand that p54 is a chain length neuro matter indeed, as well as a peptide. The two meet in synchronicity over outward-bearing matter. Inward-bearing matter meets inside chain 76.

Fulcrums of these chains lie along matter 98 and sp450, respectively. In your scientific body are the answers to all these encodings. Shift around and find. Particulate is of utmost importance in understanding all that matter can translate and transmute. Particulate founded upon chain-length 76b is of another matter entirely than pure peptide at the surface dwelling. So, in chain lengths, you will find all necessary for understanding shapeshifting and releasing of matter.

Purposeful and intended work in these areas will allow mankind technologies he has only heretofore dreamed about. But, I must warn you, these things spoken about will raise great question concerning the nature of God as we have proposed Him to be. It will be a while before mankind can sort out all these conditions within himself and his view of God, you see. So fret not in exploring what these contain.

Simeon's discourse about the molecular components that give solid matter the ability to transform into something else is what I can only now identify as a poetic discourse or riddle. Although some of the scientific terms can be named, and are defined in the glossary, Simeon's descriptions and numeric usage cannot be found in any existing scientific or medical abstract that I am aware of.

MAY 31

I continue to press Simeon for more information about the last two sessions.

Clearly, an assumption made in the face of these things could strike in a wrong direction, and that, you hold rightly. But in essence, this is all the same, and you will find out more as time rolls on. For in the essence of all things, you see, is one. And chain lengths or subdivisions of that one *do not really exist. But for now, in this time and space, they are as real for you as the next thing. And so we subdivide and categorize to death, as it were, and quite literally, in this plane. But even in death, the subdivisions of matter go on, and on.*

Now, I would like to address the formula for such chain length [matter] in the discussion before. In these chains are subdivisions of time and space, developing tomes of existence, you see, beyond and beyond. You could go on forever, and not reach an origin of source exactly.

In your world the origin of next is the origin of last. And you must put one before and after the other. But in total, there is no before and after, no cause and effect. It is all one.

But to continue, as we were discussing, of last. In tomes are volumes of material substance that comprises all matter, substrata, space, time, permanence or impermanence of objects, deterioration rates, and such. All encoded in the framework of that substance, or matter, which is contained within tomes contained within time and the perimeters thereof. So, when you subshift from one to the next, you are spacing out the framework to jettison with the next framework, and so on. In the substrata of the substrate still you have more of the essence in nature of what it means to be free of an existence within a body, or any ties to matter. But this freedom lies outward from the crux of all that pushed you inward, originally, inside the framework you now exist —not just the body, but inside earthly existence, as I am describing it. This framework in which you exist is made of harboring and holding itself into a separate strand of submatter, as long as the DNA helix can possess forthright what it proposes to be. When it is exhausted, matter ceases to exist in that same framework. But DNA coincides with what must take place on an immaterial level, the substrata found in gases around you, in molecular structures you do not yet know about. And so, you see, the collective of All That Is around you makes you stand separate from it. If this were not so, your bodies would simply melt into the air around you, or so it would appear. The strain of the helix that holds you separated is a maximum cord, refreshed daily by genetic coding. For you to ponder and wonder over these things is heedless at this time. So therefore, I will finish with this: There is a strand that stands incomplete when one breaks the length of chain matter to shift out of one's bodily form. This strand is at that time altogether catalyzed further out into time and space, becoming one with time and space, even just for an instant, without itself and within itself. This strand simply implodes upon itself and explodes outward.

Chapter Twelve

Transsets

JUNE 11

The "boys" are out and about in town, so I have some extra time tonight to explore whatever comes up.

In the right transset come proportions of thought and deed that mere mortals cannot comply. These transsets are subsets of time, space, and matter—even antimatter included, and you will find they are [formed, originated] *out of realms you have heretoward not found, not discovered, in your time and space altogether. In the hub of all that exists are transsets of time and space before you like a shroud, a shroud of fluorination that you sniff out all the days of your lives, before me, before thou, before Him, before all. In the transset of time and space and energy flows yet another course in reason for you to remark upon, and it is this: it is the outcoursing of All That Is in the specific moments of time transcribed before you as "existence" in this realm, and more so, in another. You cannot be two at once by your way of thinking, and then again, I say you can become two, or four, and that you embark upon this splitting in more ways than you can count, without even being aware of it at all. For if you were* [fully aware of these splits], *in every instance that is, you would fail to recognize any existence at all, being shrouded by the others in the places of the others, you see. And in this transset of time and space, you believe you are one body, one mind, one soul living out one life in one planetary substance, one universe among universes—and so, you see, the suggestion that you exist in many is not altogether seemingly true for you, or as you see it. But I tell you, the universe and its realms of existence are split far and wide; they course among each other in separation, and yet, in collective effort they fold into one. How you subsist in them all, a mystery to you, is really quite simple. You overlay one thought to the next as you exist in them all. All lives, all pasts, all presents, all futures. Evidence of this can be seen in your outworking of substrates and factors known already to science, in extremes. As you study these extremes in these courses that seem to lead to nothing, to nowhere, you will find the reason that you exist in all realms doing all things in all places, and yet you do not perceive them all, shrouded over by this very one. Reality therefore seems often pedestrian to you, unnecessary in its teachings, unwilling and ungiving [inflexible] in its structure. You have felt the sense of all places and times, the multiple universes and faces you wear at once, in your visions and experiences of late. They come flying forward to you in mass confusion at times, scarce enough for you to comprehend and understand, although you are willing. And so to promote this existence over all the others requires an ultra-specific focus and will into this arena you call "my life." If you should desire to explore the other patterns of existence, you only have to simply share this desire with yourself, and you will discover them one by one. It is up to you to find in your nature a chance to relax, to let go of today's, the moment's concerns, and in that very moment, transcend all that you know and feel to be true in this existence. Herein lies the discovery of transformation, transmigration, and all existences that lie without this realm. It remains to be an action of letting go of how one feels deep in his bones that anything "must be" and simply, to allow it to be something else. For the time you have left, commit to know this time, as you have committed before in other times, for it is surely as much a part of All That Is, and this is your moment to know it. Feeling desirous to travel into other realms is not necessarily a refusal to apply this technique* [of being committed to know this time]. *It is simply an understanding that, to transcend is to touch a greater reality at its seams, and then, to replace current reality with yet another perspective of just* how great *is great, and* how All *extends to all.*

I expected *transset* to be a manufactured word. However, in computer programming language, a *transset* is a tool for testing translucency. Fast becoming outdated, the term transset has been used as a resource to change the transparency of a target window, a way of assigning translucency to a window. If you take the word with this meaning and apply it to the passage above, Simeon seems to be talking about a translucency we have "set" into our existences. It becomes even more interesting when you consider the usage of the word translucency in computer terms. Translucent objects absorb some light passing through them, but not all of it. Wavelengths that can be absorbed are determined by the object's color. Indeed, translucency will influence the hue of this object, and those beyond it. By combining the color of a translucent object with those objects behind it, a designer can simulate light on the original object.

JUNE 20

It's hard for me to believe we're already wrapping up the first year of Simeon's communiqué, having covered a variety of topics, some, as questions arose, some, out of emotional need, and the rest, what subject matter arose spontaneously. While at one time I might've stored away these words in a dusty closet with my personal journals, my respect for Simeon's thoughts grew as the months rolled by, and in the end, I saw no reason to hide them. Particularly if by their exploration one or more souls can find a true and glorious smile, move toward a greater understanding of All That Is, or step up to a worthwhile challenge, my work is done. Simeon continues to expand his discourse, especially regarding a greater reality. I, for one, look forward to the journey ahead.

For it is taken among all lines of probability and possibility in time and space continuums, while they exist for you and for another, to hear, to record, and to receive. So it is among them all: the few, the many, the near, the far, the in-between. For it is of a substance heretofore not seen, not heard, not felt, not shared, herein you speak of me and from me.

This channeled, as with others, is for the eyes and ears who would see and hear, for those who would accept All in all, and receive what has been and always will be. For it is among yourselves that you shall collectively find peace, joy, and love within and without time, should you so desire it. And what man or woman among you, what creature within or without you, should host less than this? For herein ye all, is the desire for these things to be in reality, and what you strive for, you subsist in having over time and without time. For it is so. And should you feel your God has forsaken you, you may be assured He has not, nor ever will find Himself in such a state you see, for to forsake, to forget, or to ignore His creation in any fashion would bastardize all that upon inception He felt necessary for life and breath—namely you, me, and all within. So there is no lesser or more; there is not better nor worse, no matter how or what these forms may take in this avenue we call "our life," earth living, The Year of our Lord 2014, or beyond.

There is only One, and always will be One. It encases all and breathes through all, no matter what appearances may force separation into our minds. And of such a simple concept, there would be no need to drive it home, if only each man would accept. For the acceptance thereof is the difficult task at hand, while we observe entirely so much conundrum of thought and overt hatred, violence, victimization, disease, and death. Inexplicable to all and unfathomable to even one of you, quite totally, that we were formed and shaped to experience total and uninterrupted peace, love, and joy. And so, with these thoughts I must include and conclude before you, until the next, that in forward movement along these lines of tenure containing love, joy, and peace, if it is in your power to do so, continue along this path toward them all. And in seeking them, you will find. And in finding, you will share eternity. Amen.

A fish swims, birds feed themselves, the cycle continues.

—Simeon Peter

Epilogue

There's not a doubt in my mind that in certain religious circles even one hundred years from now, much of the aforementioned material will still brand me a heretic, a lunatic, or worse. And so it is with teachings that stray from the norm, or what we "know" and hold to be correct. Seven years ago I did not set out to receive these things, nor was my heart even turned this way. I was perfectly contented staking my identity inside all the other avenues life had offered me, and greatly comfortable in doing so. Simeon, I must admit, yanked me way out of my comfort zone. *Channeling? Who, me?* And, *why?*

I could set out to answer that question and spend the rest of my life doing so. And, as Simeon has pointed out, this would prove to be a colossal waste of time. He already has much more to say, building upon what he started in this book. So, against whatever backdrop life brings, particularly that of age-old skepticism, wariness, and (at best) misguided attempts to extrapolate and fit these words on for size—which can lead to the illusion of you against me and us against them—I have to hearken to Simeon's insistence that, beyond all of this—himself, myself, yourself—is a greater reality, where there is only One, and will always be One.

—Julie Rogers

Glossary

absolutism: a metaethical view that all actions may be categorized into absolute right or wrong, devoid of the context of the acts. *Graded* absolutism teaches a hierarchy of moral absolutes, such that when there exists a conflict between two absolutes, duty to obey the higher one exempts duty to the lower one, e.g. duty to God is greater than duty to fellow humans is greater than duty to property.

Alpha and the Omega, the: the first and last letters of the classical Greek alphabet, a term derived from the phrase "I Am the Alpha and the Omega" (Revelation 1:8 NIV). An appellation of God.

amalgam: derived from the Greek word *malagma*, or emollient. Any alloy mixed with another metal that remains solid or liquid at room temperature according to the proportion of mercury present, used especially in tooth cements. A mixture of different elements.

ampsig: a computer programming term, a PHP (Personal Home Page) script that dynamically generates images for use in web forums, e-mail, and blogs. Ampsigs can take various colors and forms, allowing the user to customize its appearance.

anipol(s): a Simeon-manufactured word for interpretive devices that operate using knowledge or truths that exist beyond the human capacity to reason intellectually and outside the solid matter of the human brain.

anomalous healing: treating or healing illness without a known physical curative agent. Although the following terms are not necessarily interchangeable it is sometimes known as psychic healing, spiritual healing, shamanic healing, miraculous healing, and paranormal healing.

astral projection: unlike dreaming or near-death experiences, astral projection (or soul travel) is an of out-of-body experience occurring in environments other than those in ordinary daily life, a paranormal phenomenon where the astral, or subtle body can temporarily leave the physical body to travel in other dimensions.

automatic typing/writing: the process or product of typing material that does not come from the conscious thoughts of the transcriber. Some may perform this in trance state while others remain fully aware of their surroundings.

Being: God, or, the God within; the all-encompassing Consciousness from which the universe was created. Being implies an all-permeating Consciousness—an omnipresent, omnipotent, and omniscient expression experiencing Itself from all possible viewpoints.

bilocation: also called multilocation, a term describing the ability of the body to apparently be in two or more locations at the same time. All the "selves" have the ability to interact with their surroundings in a normal manner and perform such physical acts as eating and drinking. It is distinct from astral projection and in most instances appears to be involuntary.

borderline personality disorder: a psychiatric diagnosis describing a prolonged disturbance of personality function characterized by unusual levels of instability in mood, "black and white" thinking, and chaotic and unstable interpersonal relationships, self-image, identity, and behavior.

cacophony: harsh and often meaningless mixture of discordant sounds.

canon (of Scripture): a group of Biblical texts selected by debate between [Judaistic] religious authorities as inspired by God, or expressing the authoritative history of the relationship between God and man.

carrier waves: in telecommunications, a conventional waveform (usually sinusoidal) modulated with an input signal at a certain frequency for the purpose of conveying information, e.g. radio or light.

chain length: an identifier or marker used in DNA chain termination sequencing.

chakra, Vishuddha: energetic centers lying along the axis of the human spine, not physically palpable, but repositories that mirror one's physical and psychic state of Being. The *Vishuddha* chakra represents the will and ability to express oneself through speech.

channeling: the act of receiving information, energetic influence, or mental impressions from a source apart from oneself, or another embodied mind, or any physical reality as defined by physics and psychophysiology.

chastise: modern usage implies criticism or punishment, while archaic usage infers refinement or purification.

clairaudient: also known as "clear hearing," or the act of receiving audible messages, mental impressions, tones, sounds, or thought forms from a source apart from oneself or another embodied mind, or any physical reality as defined by physics and psychophysiology. Distinguished from auditory hallucinations by the receiver's ability to differentiate the clairaudient material from physiologic reality.

clairvoyant: also known as "clear vision," or the act of receiving information about objects, locations, or physical events through means other than the known human senses, or a form of extrasensory perception.

classic channeling: the act of channeling in which an identified source claims responsibility for the information channeled.

consciousness: a term that defies simple explanation, consciousness has been loosely described as a collection of mental attributes including subjectivity, self-awareness, sentience, and the ability to perceive a relationship between oneself and one's environment. When Consciousness is capitalized, it usually refers to a universal, One, or God-consciousness.

continuum, time and space: theories that explain variation by gradual quantitative transition without abrupt changes or discontinuities. In physics, the space-time continuum model assumes space and time as part of the same continuum rather than as separate entities, whereas quantum theory includes quanta that are distinguished from continuous amounts.

craniosacral therapy: also known as CST and cranial osteopathy, it is a therapeutic method of complementary and alternative medicine used by some physical therapists, massage therapists, naturopaths, chiropractors and osteopaths. Craniosacral therapy involves gentle hands-on work with the spine and the skull and its cranial sutures, diaphragms, and the fascia.

creed, karate: according to the system of Isshin-Ryu, the statement of belief that reflects the tenants of this martial-arts system reads:

> *I come to you with only karate, empty hands.*
> *I have no weapons, but should I be forced to*
> *defend myself,*
>   *my honor, or my principals,*
> *Should it be a matter of life or death, of right or*
> *wrong,*
>   *then here are my weapons,*
> *My empty hands.*

crucifixion(s), universal: the traditional meaning of crucifixion comes from the Latin *crucifixus*, meaning "fixed to a cross." This was a widespread ancient method of execution wherein the condemned person was tied or nailed to a tree, gibbet, door, wall, or stake and left to hang until dead. Simeon's use of universal crucifixion is described as an energetic process occurring upon physical death when a person's DNA disentwines and the spirit is flung away from the body.

death: ceasing to exist in energetic form in a corporeal state.

demonic possession: assumed control over a human or animal form by a fallen angel or demon. Some symptoms include erased memories or personalities, convulsions, and syncope. The victim is said to have no control over the possessing entity, which usually can only be forced to leave by exorcism. The oldest references to demonic possession date to the times of the Sumerians.

dermatomes: areas of skin associated with pairs of dorsal roots from the spine. Pain in a dermatomic region may indicate spinal damage or neurological stenosis. The body is divided into regions that are mainly supplied by single spinal nerves, including eight cervical, twelve thoracic, five lumbar, and five sacral, all which innervate the body in patterned forms, both laterally and longitudinally.

devend: a Simeon-manufactured word defined as the act of passing into existence in this Earth plane from another dimension.

digression of the soul: as used by Simeon, it is similar to a shift in a composition or speech from the main idea to a seemingly unrelated topic (which in actuality often illustrates the speaker's point), so Simeon compares a "bunny trail" in a soul's existence that nonetheless completes the whole life, however incongruous the events may seem at the time, even those of sudden or untimely death.

dissociation: in psychiatry, symptoms such as depersonalization, derealization, and psychogenic amnesia are considered core features of dissociative disorders. Dissociation is one of a constellation of symptoms experienced by some victims of multiple forms of childhood trauma, including physical abuse and childhood sexual abuse. Studies suggest that dissociation is correlated with a history of trauma. Other symptoms in addition to anxiety, low self-esteem, depression, and chronic pain include psychic numbing, disengagement, or amnesia regarding events of trauma. Withdrawal through dissociation may provide temporary defense and coping mechanisms in cases of severe trauma.

dissociative identity disorder: a psychiatric diagnosis describing a condition in which a single person displays multiple distinct identities or personalities (known as alter egos), each with its own pattern of perceiving and interacting with the environment. The diagnosis requires that at least two personalities routinely take control of the individual's behavior with an associated amnesia that goes beyond normal forgetfulness; in addition, symptoms cannot be due to substance abuse or another medical condition. Previously listed as multiple personality disorder.

Divine, the: a broadly applied and loosely defined term, particularly when used within different faiths and belief systems, referring to a transcendent or transcendental power and its manifestations in the universe. It means "Godlike" in Latin.

druid: a member of a priestly and educated ancient Celtic class in Western Europe, Britain, and Ireland. Druids were polytheistic and animistic in worship practices. As a class they were oppressed by the Romans and had all but disappeared from written record by the second century.

eminence: modern usage implies superiority, or rank. Simeon explains his usage as one that describes mankind as radiant, or light-bearing.

energy: the electromagnetic and cyclic flux associated with all living beings, categorized in multiple combinations of yin (female) and yang (male) within Traditional Chinese Medicine. Energy manifests in waves, vibrations, or fields that fluctuate in frequency, intensity, and density.

en masse: in one group or body; collectively; all together.

entity: from an earthbound point of view, an entity is something that has a distinct and separate existence from the observer, though it need not be a material or corporeal existence. An entity may not be animate. The word *entity* can be used to imply a general sense of a being, whether or not the referent has material existence, such as a set, subset, or abstraction.

ergometric: a system that measures or tracks energy output.

essence: the real or ultimate nature of someone or something as opposed to its apparent existence; the true nature, attributes, or properties of a substance.

Essene, Essen: a member of a Jewish religious group that flourished between 250 BC and 68 AD, whose name is a Greek variant meaning "holiness." Essenes refused to participate in sacrifices and resolved instead to spiritually purify their minds. They were country dwellers and freemen who lived peacefully, communally, and meagerly, following several customs of purification, ceremonial washings, and baptisms.

factor: a phenomenon or residing element.

foal or fole, belt(s) of: as defined by Simeon, ancient pouches or bags made from tanned sheepskin.

foressence: as defined by Simeon, the sum total meaning of all spoken words available to the mind before they are actually spoken; the ability to extrapolate the meaning of not-as-yet spoken words in a time-reversed sequence.

formularies: medieval collections of models for the execution of public or private documents, or what we today call forms or templates. In Simeon's usage, formularies are possibly a way of explaining the limitations of language and therefore the human thought process.

fortnight: a unit of time equivalent to fourteen days, derived from the Old English *feorwertyne niht*, meaning "fourteen nights."

gates, chakra: these represent specific points along the Hindu or Chinese chakra circulatory system. These gates help contain or limit overall flow of chakra energy within a person's body. By opening these gates, users can surpass their own physical limits, but at the cost of extreme damage to their own bodies. In the Hindu chakra system, the eight gates are called the gates of opening, rest, life, pain, limit, view, wonder, and death.

greater reality, a: according to Simeon, a greater reality is one's internal awareness that the physical reality we inhabit is only one of many realities. With this awareness comes an expansion of consciousness.

helix, DNA: the two long polymers or nucleotides of deoxyribonucleic acid containing genetic instructions used in the development and functioning of all known living organisms and some viruses. Its backbones are made of sugars and phosphate groups joined together by ester bonds.

holistic: related to or concerned with wholes rather than the analysis of or dissection into parts; seeing the mind, body, spirit, and environment as one system.

hypnagogic: the transitional state between wakefulness and sleep, when the rational waking cognition tries to make sense of nonlinear images and associations.

hypnopompic: a term coined by spiritualist Frederick Myers for another transitional sleep state, the state of consciousness leading from sleep. It is not identical to the hypnagogic state, however, in that the hypnopompic state represents the emotional and credulous dreaming cognition trying to make sense of real world stolidity upon awakening. Depressed frontal lobe function during the first few minutes after waking causes slowed reaction time and impaired short-term memory.

illusion: a distortion of how one receives information.

impartation: transmission of information.

induction: the act of initiating a process.

interdimensions, interdimensional: in a hypothesis about unidentified flying objects (UFOs) and related events introduced by astrophysicist Jacques Vallee, UFO phenomena are regarded as visitations from other universes (or dimensions) that coexist separately alongside our own. Vallee's hypothesis also proposes that extraterrestrials are a modern manifestation of entities or phenomena that have appeared throughout and possibly before our recorded history, having been previously explained as legendary, mythological, or supernatural creatures.

interfaith: cooperative, positive interaction between people of different religious traditions and beliefs on an individual and institutional level with the goal of examining similarities between faiths, values, and commitment to service.

in toto: in Latin, meaning "on the whole," or entirely, totally.

intuitive, medical intuitive: the ability for quick and ready insight gained by a direct knowledge outside rational thought, reasoning, or inference; in alternative medicine, a person who uses intuition to determine the root cause (versus diagnosis) of a physical or emotional condition. Medical intuitive healers usually treat from a holistic viewpoint, encouraging their clients to participate in their own healing.

kabbalah: a Hebrew term meaning "receiving." Kabbalists adhere to an esoteric (known by a select few) school of thought regarding the mystical and metaphysical aspects of Judaism, exploring the inner meanings of traditional rabbinic literature (the Tanakh and the Zohar).

karate, Isshin-Ryu: founded in the 1950s by Master Tatsuo Shimabuku, Isshin-Ryu karate has roots that date back 500 years. It is derived from several older classical styles of karate and continues to be taught in schools throughout the world today.

kenosis: a Greek term meaning "emptiness." In eastern theology, it is the concept of bypassing one's conceptualization to experience the formless truth of God. In western theology, it is the concept of self-emptying one's own will in order to become entirely receptive to God's perfect will.

klipah: a kabbalistic term that refers to metaphysical barriers in planetary existence that block light and prevent human souls from shining at their greatest brilliance.

levitation: a phenomenon of psychokinesis (PK) in which objects, people, or animals are lifted and suspended in the air without any detectable physical means. This phenomenon can occur in mediumship, shamanism, trance, and mystical rapture. Some cases of levitation appear to be spontaneous, while spiritual or magical adepts are said to be able to control the phenomenon consciously. In order to levitate from Earth, a vertical force must be applied directly upward and equivalent to gravitational forces on the object. In addition, any displacement of a levitating object must be stabilized by a returning force. Stable levitation can be naturally achieved by magnetic or aerodynamic forces. Scientists have discovered a way to levitate micro-objects by manipulating the Casimir-Polder force, which normally causes objects to stick together by quantum force.

life breath: or *pranayama*, is a universal energy or life force omnipresent in nature, a portion of which resides in the human body. Yogic practices teach that prana lies dormant as potential energy or *kundalini* in the first, or *Muladhara,* chakra. Pranayama is awakened by the dynamics of yogic breathing, which includes slow and complete exhalation.

lines of thought, or sine waves: a Simeon-concocted concept identifying thought as circular, or a sine wave (sinusoid), a function that occurs often in mathematics, physics, signal processing, audition, electrical engineering, and many other fields. A sine wave's most basic form is: $y(t) = A \cdot \sin(\omega t + \theta)$. Sine waves are important in physics because they retain their wave shape when added to other sine waves of the same frequency and arbitrary phase. The sine wave is the result when one stretches out the algebraic model of the rotation of a wheel.

madrigal: a secular vocal music composition written for two- to eight voices during the Renaissance and early Baroque eras. By nature it was polyphonic, through-composed, and unaccompanied by musical instruments. Early examples date from Italy in the 1520s, as well as England and Germany. The madrigal was the most important secular form of music of its time.

maileron: a Simeon-manufactured word defined as the act of receiving channeled messages by wave impulses that have a rolling pattern, which presents the need of an aileron device, speaking metaphorically, to sort through the signals and make them out as separate words.

manipulation, osteopathic: osteopathic manipulation therapy (OMT) is a whole system of evaluation and treatment by trained osteopathic physicians, the therapeutic application of manual pressure or force, and not simply or exclusively the realignment of joints. OMT can be used as modality to treat many forms of disease, since osteopathy asserts that problems originating in the spinal column can affect the nerves that radiate outward, affecting all bodily organs and various systemic processes.

mental construct: a philosophy which teaches that the constructs of time and space would not exist in the same way if human consciousness finds a new way to observe, accept, and interact with them.

mental field: viewing the mind as more than just the electromagnetic patterns in the brain, but a field or fields that interrelate and interconnect with all matter and energy within its realm of influence. Fields are not matter, but rather, matter is energy bound within those fields.

metaphysical: pertaining to a branch of philosophy dealing with aspects of the ultimate nature of reality, beyond that which is perceptible to the physical senses.

metrical: relating to or composed in poetic meter.

metricular, metricularity: substances that help distinguish or identify form or matter.

metrigal: a Simeon-manufactured word defined within the text as the point in which all things consume each other, or the meeting point of all energetic varieties and tonal frequencies.

microparticle: a particle between 0.1 and 100 mm in size. Commercially available microparticles include those made of glass, latex, polystyrene, various metals, and magnetic materials. Microparticles are found in pollen, very fine sand, and dust.

miscreate, miscreation: to make badly; as used in *A Course In Miracles*, miscreation is man's egoistic attempts to fashion the world he perceives around himself within the limitations of his own physical senses, therefore living in the illusion that ego is real.

mitigation: to moderate a quality or condition's force or intensity; to alleviate or become milder.

molecular: study at the molecular level, a molecule being a sufficiently stable and electrically neutral group of at least two atoms held together in a definite arrangement by very strong chemical bonds. A unit of two or more atoms held together by covalent bonds.

morphic field: a field within and around a morphic unit which organizes its characteristic structure and pattern of activity. It includes morphogenetic, behavioral, social, cultural, and mental fields. Shaped and stabilized by morphic resonance, these fields contain a kind of cumulative memory and tend to become increasingly habitual.

morphogenesis: coming into being (form).

morphogenetic field: as theorized by biologist Rupert Sheldrake, these are fields that play a causal role in morphogenesis. First proposed in the 1920s, the term is now widely used by developmental biologists, but the nature of morphogenetic fields has remained obscure. On the hypothesis of formative causation, they are regarded as morphic fields stabilized by morphic resonance.

mystic, mysticism: derived from the Greek *mystikos*, a mystic is an initiate of a mystery religion or religions in the pursuit of communion with, identity with, or conscious awareness of an ultimate reality, divinity, spiritual truth, or God through direct experience, intuition, or insight. Mystics are often treated skeptically due to their emphasis on personal experience over doctrine. Their teachings may be regarded by skeptics or mainstream adherents as mere obfuscation, though mystics suggest they are offering clarity of a different order or kind.

neuromatic: a Simeon-manufactured word, probably pertaining to neuro matter.

neuro matter: a lay word for nerve tissue in general, including that consisting of grey or white brain and spinal cord matter. Gray matter, a major component of the central nervous system, consists of nerve cell bodies, glial cells, capillaries, and short nerve cell extensions. It is also composed of cell bodies, as opposed to white matter, which is composed of cell axons. Its brownish-gray color comes from the capillaries and neuronal cell bodies. Gray matter is distributed at the surface level of the cerebral hemispheres and cerebellum, as well as in the deeper cerebral, cerebellar, and spinal areas. Its function is to route sensory and motor stimulus to the central nervous system. White matter is one of three main solid components of the central nervous system, composed of bundles of myelinated nerve cell processes, or lipids. White matter connects various gray matter areas of the brain to each other, serving as a conduit for messages. White matter, unlike gray matter, continues to develop late in life.

neurons: responsive cells in the nervous system that process and transmit information by chemical signals. They are the core components of the brain, the vertebrate spinal cord, the invertebrate ventral nerve cord, and the peripheral nerves.

nonmatter: natural phenomenon and forces (such as gravity and electromagnetic radiation), that, while they do not exist in solid form, can interact with solid forms (matter).

occult: the study of occult or hidden wisdom. Occultism can involve magic, alchemy, extrasensory perception, astrology, spiritualism, and numerology. Some occultists adhere to ancient religious beliefs that originated in the eastern Mediterranean area such as Gnosticism, Hermeticism, Thelema, and Neo-paganism.

open channeling: the act of receiving information from an unidentifiable source, as coming from another dimension or level of reality than the physical world or from one's own psychological self, conscious or unconscious. This type of channeling usually occurs in a completely ordinary way, in the form of creative or intuitive ideas or inspiration. It is a universal phenomenon, available to everyone, occurring in the mainstream of daily life.

osteopathic physician: a physician who practices osteopathic medicine, a unique form of medical care started in 1874 by Andrew Taylor Still, M.D., D.O. Dissatisfied with the effectiveness of 19th century medicine, Still believed that many of the therapies of his day were useless or even harmful. Dr. Still was one of the first in his time to study the attributes of good health so that he could better understand the process of disease. He developed a philosophy of medicine based on ideas that date back to ancient Greek and Oriental therapies, focusing on the functioning unity of all body parts. Dr. Still also identified a healthy musculoskeletal system as a key element of good health. He recognized the body's ability to heal itself and stressed preventive medicine, eating properly, and keeping fit. In today's terms, osteopathic physicians evaluate each patient's individual health risks— such as smoking, high blood pressure, excessive cholesterol levels, stress, spiritual and emotional isolation, and other risk factors.

ovend: a Simeon-manufactured word meaning the act of passing out of existence in this Earth plane to another dimension.

particle: a term identified as a misnomer today, because the dynamics of particle physics are governed by quantum mechanics. As such, what were once identified as particles also exhibit wave-particle duality, displaying particle-like behavior under certain experimental conditions and wave-like behavior under others. Following the convention of particle physicists, "elementary particles" refer to objects such as electrons and photons, with the understanding that these "particles" display wave-like properties as well.

particulate: tiny particles of solid or liquid suspended in a gas. Some occur naturally, originating from volcanoes, dust storms, forest and grassland fires, living vegetation, and sea spray.

particum: particum is a Partiki unit, but Particum Partiki is slower moving and contains half of the electrotonal (electrified sound thrust or force) of its twin Partiki subunit. Partiki subunits that pulsate more slowly and appear in conjunction with the Partika are called Particum, and they set the pulsation rhythm through which Partiki units will group to form particles manifestation within the unified fields of the 15-dimensional time matrix. The 15-dimensional structure of our time matrix allows us to explore five distinct stations of identity or platforms of perception: Incarnate, Soul, Oversoul, Avatar and Rishi.

partite: divided into parts that are used or combined together, usually into a specified number of parts, such as a tripartite agreement.

pathfinder: one's own internal components of a wayshower, which is a prophet or enlightened one who by virtue of evolutionary progress can lead humanity through spiritual development.

peptide: short polymers formed from the linking, in a defined order, of amino acids. The link between one amino acid residue and the next is known as an amide bond or a peptide bond. Proteins are polypeptide molecules. The distinction is that peptides are short and polypeptides are long.

Pharisee: one of at least four major schools of thought within the Jewish religion around the first century that were most prominently in opposition to the Sadducee sect. They were also one of several successor groups of first-century Hasidim, an anti-Hellenistic Jewish movement. Fundamentally, the Pharisees practiced a form of Judaism that extended beyond the Temple, applying Jewish law to mundane activities in order to sanctify the everyday world.

phoneme: the smallest posited structural unit that distinguishes meaning in speech. They are not the physical segments themselves, but, in theoretical terms, cognitive abstractions or categorizations of them. Example: the /p/ sound in cap, piece, and splendor.

phylactery belts: a Jewish covenant and prayer belt received after Bar Mitzvah, with boxes containing Hebrew text on vellum.

pineal gland: a small endocrine gland shaped like a pine cone that resides near the center of the brain, tucked between its two hemispheres. It produces melatonin, a hormone that affects the modulation of wake/sleep patterns and photoperiodic (seasonal) functions.

plane: in theories of emanation, as in Neoplatonism, an emergent state, level, or region of reality, emanating from the Divine and culminating in the physical plane. The incarnate state on earth represents one of several possible planes.

precognition, precognitive: a form of extrasensory perception where one perceives information about places or events through paranormal means before they happen. The related term "presentiment" refers to information about future events, said to be perceived as emotions. Both forms are used by mediums and clairvoyants.

protons: a small particle with an electric charge of +1 elementary charge. Often found as a subatomic particle in the nucleus of an atom, a proton is also stable in an ionic form, also known as the hydrogen ion, H^+. It is composed of two up-quarks and one down-quark.

psychic: the ability to perceive things hidden from the normal senses through extrasensory perception, or a reference to those people who have such abilities.

psychic connections: interaction with psychic or paranormal activity.

psychic invasion: unwanted intrusion by a person or entity into one's personal space, which can result in discomfort, confusion, pain, and in extreme cases illness.

psychic reading: using extrasensory perception, a person designated as psychic receives helpful information for a client. A good reading gives accurate insight, practical advice, as well as hope and inspiration. It also encourages self-examination, highlights a client's gifts and abilities, while respecting the free will and power to change.

Qigong, Qigong energy healing: a wide variety of traditional Chinese cultivation practices that involve methods of accumulating and working with Qi, or circulating energy through meridian channels in the body. Qigong doesn't always involve movement or regulated breathing. Use of special methods of focusing the mind on particular energy centers in and around the body are common in the higher levels of Qigong. Qigong can be practiced for health purposes or therapeutic intervention. It can be incorporated in a medical profession, spiritual path, or as a component of Chinese martial arts.

quadrant: in accordance with integral theory, at least four primary dimensions or perspectives exist through which we can experience the world: subjective, inter-subjective, objective, and inter-objective. In the subjective quadrant is the world of individual, interior experiences: thoughts, emotions, memories, states of mind, perceptions, and immediate sensations, or the "I" space. In the inter-subjective quadrant is the world of collective, interior experiences: shared values, meanings, language, relationships, and cultural background, or the "we" space. In the objective quadrant is the world of individual, exterior things: the material body (including the brain) and anything that can be seen or touched in time and space, or the "it" space. In the inter-objective quadrant is the world of collective, exterior things: systems, networks, technology, government, and the natural environment, or the "it" space.

quantum theory: a branch of theoretical physics that developed in the early 1900s as an endeavor to understand the fundamental properties of matter. The study of quantum mechanics began with observing interactions of matter and radiation. Certain results could not be explained by classical mechanics or the theory of electromagnetism. Physicists were puzzled by the nature of light in particular. Spectral lines had been discovered earlier by Joseph von Fraunhofer (1787–1826). These were systematically cataloged for various substances, yet no one could explain why these spectral lines were there or why they would differ for each substance. Out of this, quantum mechanics developed as a study of mechanical systems whose dimensions are close to the atomic scale, such as molecules, atoms, electrons, protons, and other subatomic particles. Quantum theory therefore generalizes classical mechanics to provide accurate descriptions for many previously unexplained phenomena.

rather-bes: a Simeon-manufactured word explained as the basic human desire to create and change.

reading—*see* **psychic reading.**

reincarnation, reincarnational: an ancient belief and central tenet within the majority of Indian religious traditions (Hinduism, Yoga, Vaishnavism, Shaivism, Jainism, Sikhism, Buddhism, Paganism, Spiritism, Sufism, Gnostic Christianity, Esoteric Christianity, as well as in Greek and Kabbalistic philosophies). Reincarnation, which literally means "to be made flesh again," is a metaphysical belief that some essential part of a living being survives death to be reborn into a new body, be it spirit, soul, higher or true Self, a Divine spark, or the "I." A new personality is developed during each lifetime in the physical world, but some part of the original soul remains constant throughout successive lives.

releasement: the act of releasing, as from confinement or obligation.

sayonara: Japanese goodbye, translating "if it must be so."

Second Coming, the: in Christian teachings, the Second Coming, or Second Advent, is the anticipated return of Jesus from Heaven to Earth, an event that will fulfill certain aspects of Messianic prophecy according to the Holy Bible, such as the general resurrection of the dead, the last judgment, the full establishment of the Kingdom of God on Earth, and the Messianic Age. Views about the nature of this return vary among Christian denominations.

Self, whole, true, or Higher, Highest Self: a term found within multiple belief systems meaning an eternal, conscious, and intelligent Being. The term has been popularized by New Age and newer religious movements (Neo-paganism). It is used by many different groups and has multiple meanings and interpretations. Each individual incarnates or reincarnates into bodily form from its authentic Self, Being sent to garner experience on the third dimension, in this case, planet Earth. When an individual dies, the energy stream from the Self is withdrawn from the physical body. The Self is always connected to each individual incarnation and guides the individual throughout life. The individuated mind/body energy stream completes its experience and then absorbs back into its Self. It is also referred to as the "I Am" presence. All Selves are regarded as One, being part of Universal Consciousness.

self-hypnosis: the word "hypnosis" stems from *hypnos*, the Greek word for sleep. An intriguing, often ambiguous state when the brain sends out an alpha wave, where a person's attention is focused on a single objective while awareness of peripheral noises or events blur in the background. Self-hypnosis occurs to most individuals at least twice daily, also labeled "daydreaming" or "preoccupation." It occurs most readily and frequently when the body is given some simple, repetitive task, such that one's focus becomes so narrowed that other stimuli in the environment are "softened."

sessions: semipermanent interactive information exchanges, dialogues, conversations, or meetings between two or more communicators or communicating devices. Established communication sessions may involve more than one message in each direction. A session is typically stateful, meaning that at least one of the communicating parts will save or record the information about the session history.

shalom: a Hebrew word meaning peace, completeness, and welfare that can be used idiomatically to mean both *hello* and *goodbye*.

shapeshifting: a common reference in mythology, wizardology, and folklore, as well as in science fiction and fantasy. In its broadest sense, it is a metamorphosis, or change in the physical form or shape of a person or animal. It involves such physical changes as alterations of age, gender, race, or general appearance, including therianthropy, a shift from human to animal, plant, or inanimate object, and vice versa. The most important aspect of shapeshifting, thematically, is whether the transformation is voluntary. When a form is taken on involuntarily, the thematic effect is one of confinement and restraint, whereas voluntary shapeshifting becomes a means of escape and liberation.

shekhinah: derived from a Hebrew verb, the word literally means *to settle, inhabit,* or *dwell,* as frequently used in the Tanakh, or Hebrew Bible.

Sicarri: literally, "the dagger men," an extremist splinter group to first-century Jewish Zealots or insurgents who concealed *sicae,* or small daggers, under their cloaks. At popular assemblies they were known to stab Romans or Roman sympathizers and lament ostentatiously after the deed in order to blend into the crowd and escape detection.

siglet: a dashboard widget in computers that communicates with ampsig, feeding it the information to display screen. It sends information about updates as well as how long the computer has been running.

somatic dysfunction: an impaired or altered function of the musculoskeletal system diagnosed by physical examination. It commonly presents as tissue texture change, asymmetry, restriction, or tenderness that is frequently associated reciprocally with visceral illness. The resolution of either can aid in the resolution of the other.

Source, the: the originating, creative source of everything physical and metaphysical, also called by many other names including God, Gaia, Allah, Om, I Am, or All That Is.

Spirit, spirit: Spirit (capitalized) refers to the theories of a unified spirituality, universal consciousness, and some concepts of Deity. All spirits together form a greater unity, Spirit, which maintains an ultimate, unified, non-dual awareness or force of life that combines or transcends all individual units of consciousness. The term spirit (lowercase) is used to refer to one who is transcendent and therefore metaphysical in nature, as well as a natural part of mind or consciousness.

subatomic: a particle that is an elementary or composite particle smaller than an atom. Subatomic particles include the atomic constituents electrons, protons, and neutrons.

submatter: a scientifically unproven spectrum of 3-D matter composed of adamantine particles following a different set of physical laws and oscillating at very high frequencies.

subshift: in mathematics, subshifts are used to model dynamical systems (a mathematical formalization for any fixed "rule" which describes the time dependence of a point's position in its ambient space). In particular, subshifts are the objects of study in symbolic dynamics and ergodic theory (theory that studies dynamical systems with an invariant measure and related problems). They also describe the set of all possible sequences executed by a finite state machine. The most widely studied shift spaces are the subshifts of a finite type.

substrate: in biochemistry, a substrate is a molecule upon which an enzyme acts. Enzymes catalyze chemical reactions involving the substrate(s). The substrate binds with the enzyme's active site, and an enzyme-substrate complex is formed. The substrate is broken down into a product and is released from the active site. The active site is now free to accept another substrate molecule.

substructure: in universal algebra, an (induced) substructure or (induced) subalgebra is a structure whose domain is a subset of that of a bigger structure, and whose functions and relations are the traces of the functions and relations of the bigger structure. Some examples of subalgebras are subgroups, submonoids, subrings, subfields, subalgebras of algebras over a field, or induced subgraphs. Shifting the point of view, the larger structure is called an extension or a superstructure of its substructure.

sukhasana: known as the "easy pose," *sukhasana* is a basic cross-legged posture used in meditation and yogic breathing practice. Inherently it is less stable than the *swastikana* position and is better performed with back support. One foot may be placed slightly in front for additional balance. In Hatha practice, the legs are alternated daily.

sulfide: refers to several types of chemical compounds containing sulfur in its lowest oxidation number of -2. It is the dianion that exists in strongly alkaline aqueous solutions formed from H_2S or alkali metal salts.

telepathy: from the Greek word *tele* meaning "distant" and *patheia* meaning "to be affected by," the term describes the transfer of information from thoughts or feelings between individuals by means other than the five physical senses.

tenure, waves of, or lines of: a Simeon-concocted concept, probably based upon the idea of expansion of thought similar to that found in academic tenure, which is intended to guarantee one's right to academic freedom. Tenure protects teachers and researchers if they disagree from prevailing opinion, or openly differ with authorities of any sort, or spend time on unpopular topics. Tenure makes original ideas more likely to surface by giving scholars an intellectual autonomy to investigate problems and solutions about which they are most passionate, and report their honest conclusions.

theory, quantum—*see* **quantum theory.**

third eye, the: also known as the inner eye, a mystical and esoteric term referring to the *Ajna* chakra, which, combined with the pineal gland becomes the gateway leading to spaces of higher consciousness. It is often associated with visions, clairvoyance, precognition, and out-of-body experiences.

thought, lines or sine waves—*see* **lines of thought**

tonal frequency: along a spectrum of possible tones, the lowest frequency, pitch, or note named is called the *fundamental frequency*. In western music, instruments are normally tuned to A = 440 Hz. Other significant frequencies, called overtones of the fundamental frequency, may include harmonics and partials. Tonal frequencies also include those pitches along the spectrum that are inaudible to the human ear. Therapeutic exposure to certain tonal frequencies is used in Qigong and other alternative medicines to heal disease.

Traditional Chinese Medicine (TCM): a range of traditional medical practices originating thousands of years ago in China through meticulous observation of nature, the cosmos, and the human body. TCM practice includes treatments such as herbal medicine, acupuncture, dietary therapy, Tui Na and Shiatsu massage, and Qigong healing.

transmigrate: to cause to go from one state of existence or place to another, or to pass upon death from one body or being to another.

transmute: to change or alter in form, appearance, or nature, especially to a higher form; to subject an element to transmutation.

transset: a tool in computer programming for testing translucency. It is used as a resource to change the transparency of a target window, a way of assigning translucency to a window.

triloquy: a soliloquy for three with strong melodic and thematic orientation and some nontraditional harmonies.

trines: a group of three. In astrology it is the aspect of two planets that are 120 degrees apart, often thought of as an astrologically (aspected) favorable position of two celestial bodies.

Tui Na: known in Chinese as "push-pull" massage, it is a form of Chinese manipulative therapy often used in conjunction with acupuncture, moxibustion, herbalism, and Qigong. It also incorporates acupressure, a modality of Chinese medicine designed to bring the body into balance.

Upanishads: thought to have been composed by philospher and commentator Shankara, these Hindu scriptures constitute the core teachings of Vedanta. They do not belong to any particular period of Sanskrit literature. The Upanishads exert an important influence on the rest of Hindu and Indian philosophy and are considered one of the 100 most influential books ever written.

vector: a geometric object that has magnitude and direction, as well as orientation along a given direction. It is frequently represented by a line segment with a definite direction, or graphically as an arrow, connecting an initial point A with a terminal point B. In linear algebra, a coordinate vector is an explicit representation of a vector in an abstract vector space as an ordered list of numbers or, equivalently, as an element of the coordinate space F^n.

vend: a Simeon-manufactured word meaning to pass through time and space.

vibratory thermal energy: the total internal kinetic energy of an object due to the random motion of its atoms and molecules.

waves, sine—*see* **lines of thought or sine waves.**

Wei Qi: in Traditional Chinese Medicine, it is considered the body's field of superficial defense, or the immune system.

Yahweh, YHVH: a proposed vocalization of the Hebrew tetragrammaton commonly translated as Jehovah. Among observant Jews it is a name believed to be too sacred to be uttered out loud.

yoga, Tibetan, raja: also known as royal yoga, a principal focus of its rites are concerned with cultivation of the mind through meditation (*dhana*) in order to further one's acquaintance with reality and achieve liberation.

zodiac, Chinese: a twelve-year astrological cycle, with each year named after one of the original twelve animals. Each animal has a different personality and different characteristics. The animal is believed to be the main factor in a person's life that gives that person's individual traits, success, and predisposition to happiness. It is a pure calendrical cycle, with no equivalent constellations like those of the occidental zodiac.

Index

About Julie Rogers

Transcribing for Simeon Peter, **Julie Rogers** is an award-winning inspirational writer and speaker. Her articles have been published in such magazines as *Coping with Cancer, Daily Meditation,* and the anthology *Writes of Passage: Every Woman has a Story!* She is author of the self-help book *Happy Tails: How Pets Can Help You Survive Divorce.*

Some of her writing awards include the Writer's Digest Grand Prize award in 1999 and *Fade In* magazine's semifinalist screenwriting award in 2005.

Rogers began her studies in Medical Qigong at China Academy of Chinese Medical Sciences, Bejing, after a seventeen-year career as an athletic trainer. She is an ordained interfaith minister (*St. John's University,* Tennessee), certified in spiritual counseling and hypnosis. She is also certified in neuromuscular massage (*St. John Neuromuscular Pain Relief Institute,* Florida), chakra healing, therapeutic nutrition, and reflexology (*American Institute of Holistic Theology,* Alabama).

For more information about Simeon Peter, visit
www.divinecontracts.com

www.ingramcontent.com/pod-product-compliance
Lightning Source LLC
Chambersburg PA
CBHW030917090426
42737CB00007B/226